D0717417

BECOMING A CHRISTIAN

A Manual for Communicant Classes

By

LEWIS JOSEPH SHERRILL

and

HELEN HARDWICKE SHERRILL

RICHMOND: JOHN KNOX PRESS

Seventh Printing, 1959

PRINTED IN U.S.A.
COPYRIGHT 1943, JOHN KNOX PRESS, RICHMOND, VIRGINIA
6437—(1)—3735

CONTENTS

Part Three—For the Pastor

Part Four—For the Parents

PREFACE

THIS little book is written for persons who are preparing to make public profession of faith in Jesus Christ, for pastors who have classes in communicant instruction, and for parents who wish to supplement the pastor's instruction by home teaching. We hope it may prove helpful to many, regardless of age and experience, as they consider the meaning of this greatest of all decisions. But as we wrote, we thought chiefly of boys and girls.

We have put the material in four parts so that it may be used in classes where that is desired.

Part One consists of six brief chapters, so prepared that they may be studied by the boys and girls during the class period, under the guidance of the pastor. If the minister wishes, he may also assign one of these lessons at a time, to be read at home before coming to class. These six lessons lead up to the decision to make profession of faith in Christ as Saviour and Lord, and to the decision to be a member of the church.

Part Two has seven other brief chapters for study by the boys and girls after the communicants' class has ended. It is not enough to become a Christian, for one needs also to grow as a Christian. The purpose of these seven chapters for continued study is to show how that growth may take place.

Part Three is for the pastor who teaches the communicants' class. The minister of course should supplement or change any of the pupil material as he may see fit. But for those who wish to use it, this part contains suggestions for supervising the pupils' study of the six lessons in Part One, while the class is in session.

Part Four is for parents, especially for those who may wish to guide the continued study of their own sons and daughters, at home, after the pastor's class has come to a close.

When this booklet is used as a text for a pastor's class, each pupil should have his own copy, which he will keep after the study is finished. Unless the lessons of Part One are assigned for home study, the books should be left at the church until the class has come to an end. Then they should be taken home, a note or message being sent to the parents, asking them to co-operate by helping in the continued home study.

While this material has been planned for use as just described, many adaptations are possible. For example, a minister who wishes to conduct a communicants' class having less than six class periods, might select five, or even four, lessons from Part One; although we recommend using at least the six as given. One who is not content to end the study with six lessons could readily adapt any or all of the lessons for home study and thus lengthen the course to as many as thirteen periods.

We have written specifically for those who, in professing their faith in Christ, are preparing to take up the rights and responsibilities of membership in a Presbyterian church. For that reason we have tried, throughout, to keep in mind the "children of the covenant." Out of our own parenthood we have come to understand something of the richness of this conception, both for parents and for children. We have also seen, throughout the Church, how easily this great experience of childhood in a Christian home can be overlooked when a child comes to make his own decision. But we are mindful of the many backgrounds from which children and youth come, and we have sought to make the material equally suited to the circumstances of those who may not have been children of the church from their birth.

Lewis J. Sherrill

Helen Hardwicke Sherrill

Louisville, Kentucky

Part One

FOR THE CLASS

I

FOLLOWERS OF CHRIST

The Story of Jesus

JESUS was born in the little town of Bethlehem. The Christmas stories and songs which we love so well, tell of his birth and of the days when he was a tiny babe. God was in a special and different way his Father, and Mary was his mother. Joseph was Mary's husband.

While Jesus was growing up, the family lived in Nazareth. There were four other brothers, James, Joses, Judas, and Simon. He had at least two sisters. Joseph was a carpenter, and Jesus worked in the shop, learning the carpenter's trade. In his home he learned the beautiful religious customs of the Jews. In the synagogue, a place something like a church, he learned to worship, going there each Sabbath with his family. At home and in the synagogue he learned that part of the Bible which we now call the Old Testament. He played, worked, and grew as other boys did. And he probably went to school to a rabbi who taught him the Jewish religious law.

The people in the land where Jesus lived were far from being happy. Their country had once been free, and they remembered the glory of those days, but now their nation was ruled by the Romans who had conquered it.

13

Roman officials and soldiers were everywhere. The Jews had to obey the Romans but could not respect them. But that was not all. Taxes were high, so high that when anyone in Jesus' family earned three pennies, he had to pay about one penny of it for taxes. Wages were low. Food was scarce. Work was hard. Discontent was spreading among the people. Riots frequently broke out, but as soon as trouble started, the Roman soldiers were on hand to stop it.

The people longed for deliverance. They thought of it day and night, while they worked and when they prayed. They talked of it when they met in little groups.

For many years the Jews had been expecting a Deliverer, a Redeemer, to arise among them. They called him "the Messiah." They expected the Messiah to be a special messenger and servant of God, who would deliver the people. As their troubles grew, they waited for the Messiah, the Redeemer, with even greater longing.

But when they talked about the Messiah, they could not agree among themselves as to the way he would deliver them from their troubles and redeem them. Some believed the Messiah would gather an army of Jewish soldiers, and lead this army in revolt against the Romans. Then, they thought, the Jews could be an independent nation, and be free again. But others had quite a different idea. They thought God's power would break forth from heaven and set them free. They looked for God to send an army of angels, with swords of fire, so that the Roman army would flee in terror. Then the Messiah could be made King of the Jews, and they would be redeemed.

When Jesus was very young he seems to have known that he was God's Son, and that he had a special work to do. When he spoke of it as a boy of twelve, he said, "I must be about my Father's business." Probably he was coming to know, then, that he was the Messiah, the Deliverer or Redeemer whom the people were expecting. We do not know whether he became sure when he was a little boy, or when he was a youth, or only after he was a man. But at last he became perfectly sure that he was the Messiah. He knew he was the one who should be the Deliverer.

But how should he do it? We can imagine he thought of that question again and again. Should he raise an army and lead them to fight against the Romans? He knew that many courageous men would respond any day he sent out the call. But perhaps just at the moment when he would think of that, he would remember the things he had seen in the city of Sepphoris, not far from Nazareth. A man named Judas had started a revolution when Jesus was a boy. He had used the city of Sepphoris for the headquarters of his army. But the Romans quickly put down the rebellion, burned the city of Sepphoris to the ground, and led away the people of the city to be slaves.

If Jesus should raise an army to set his people free, would it end like that? If he thought of raising an army to deliver his people, he must also have thought of the men who would be wounded, and the men who would be killed, and the children who would be left without fathers, and the women who would be made widows, and the homes that would be burned, and the people who would be made slaves. Could there not be some other way to save his people?

Then he must have turned to think of the hope which some of the other Jews had, that God would send an army of angels with fiery swords to deliver them from the Romans, and set up the Messiah as King of the Jews. He knew God had the power to do that. Perhaps he prayed, again and again, hoping to know for certain whether that was what God wished.

How it came into his mind we do not know, but at last he became sure that God did not wish him to be a Redeemer who would raise an army, nor a Redeemer who would wait for angels to come from heaven to put him on the throne and keep him there, but that God wished him to deliver and redeem his people by helping them to live so they could be free within. They could not be free unless God was the King of their hearts. And God could not be King of their hearts unless they loved God as their Father, and loved one another.

Then Jesus began to tell the people the things he was certain of, in his own heart. He announced, "The kingdom of God is at hand." When the Jews heard him proclaim that, they knew instantly that he also meant to say, "The Messiah is here! The Deliverer, the Redeemer, the Saviour, whom you have expected so long, has come!"

He went throughout the country, proclaiming that message wherever men would listen. They came for miles to hear him. He taught them, constantly trying to help them understand "the Kingdom of God," how they could enter it, and how they should live as citizens of that Kingdom. He healed many who were sick, and performed works which made men wonder at his power.

He called certain men to follow him as he went through the country. They went with him, helped him in his work, and learned from him as he taught them of God who is our Father.

He became so popular that many expected him to raise an army to set the country free. But always he refused, for the freedom which he wished men to have was possible no matter whether Romans or Jews governed the country. But many, when they saw what he meant, turned away and left him. His teaching did not please those who expected the Messiah to set up his throne and drive the Romans out. So some of the people who considered themselves patriots turned against him.

And his teaching did not please the leaders of the Jewish religion any better. Those leaders were the teachers of the Jewish law, and were called by such names as scribes, Pharisees, and Sadducees. They taught the people that God wished them to keep a great many laws. Jesus taught that God wished most of all that people should love him, and should love one another. These leaders thought that Jesus' teaching was unfavorable to the Jewish religion and was undermining the confidence of the people in their religion. So they, too, turned against him.

Jesus saw that neither the patriots nor the religious leaders were willing for the people to be delivered as he wished to deliver them. And he knew what that meant for him. He knew they would kill him unless he changed his teaching. But he knew he was teaching them the way God wished them to be saved, and he would not consent to change his teaching just to please the patriots and the religious leaders.

So he began to prepare his disciples for what was sure to come. He began to tell them that he must die. In the Last Supper with them, he told them that his body would be broken for them, and his blood would be shed for them. They tried to understand, but they could not fully grasp what he meant.

At last the religious leaders became so bitter against him that they brought him to trial. He could have escaped, but he would not run away from danger. He could have raised an army even then to defend him, but he would not ask an army to save him from danger. He had taught that the way of love is the way men should live, and he would not go back on it, even when death faced him.

When he came to trial, at first they could not make out

any serious charge against him. But then Pilate asked him, "Art thou the King of the Jews?" Jesus knew he was the Messiah, and when they asked him that, he could not say, "No, I am not King of the Jews." But he knew that if he said, "Yes," the Romans would think he intended to set up a throne in Jerusalem. He knew they would count the answer "Yes" as treason to the Roman Empire. And he knew that treason was punished by death. *He* knew that when he said he was the King of the Jews, he wished to be King of men's hearts, and not the King of the country. But he knew that the Roman officers would never understand *that*. And he understood fully that if he said, "Yes," they would put him to death.

But the answer "Yes" was the truth. God had sent him into the world as the Messiah, to be the King of men's hearts. He had lived for that purpose, and he could not deny it now.

Pilate asked him, "Art thou the King of the Jews?" And Jesus replied, "Thou sayest it." That meant, "Yes."

With that they set upon him, beat him, mocked him, spat upon him, put a crown of thorns on his head, and led him out to crucify him. The Son of God, the Messiah, died on the cross, hung there between two thieves. Over his head they put the words, "The King of the Jews." And when he was dead, they buried him in a stone cave, sealed the door, put guards over the tomb, and left him.

But even death could not hold him. The third day he arose again from the dead. He was seen alive by many witnesses. But after forty days he was seen no more in the body, for he had returned to be with his Father.

But his Spirit, which he had promised to his disciples, has never left the world. Jesus had scarcely gone away when men and women began to feel his Spirit among them, more powerfully than they had ever done before. They began to understand now that they were redeemed, saved, by his death. They began to become his followers by the hundreds and by the thousands. And we shall learn more of that story, for it is a story which has gone on until this day.

Followers of Jesus

When Jesus began to teach the people, he called followers to go with him. He took them with him as he went through the country. These followers were often called "disciples," which means "learners." They were apprentices with Jesus, learning from him about the Kingdom of God, and learning how to do the work of that Kingdom.

Jesus expected much of his disciples.

He expected *trust*. He wished them to believe the things he taught them, and they would believe these things if they trusted him.

He expected *loyalty*. He knew his disciples would be invited to leave him and follow other leaders, or sometimes they might wish to return home. He needed men who would be as loyal to him as he was to his Father in heaven.

He expected *learning*. He had much to teach them. He could not teach any persons except those who were eager to learn more.

He expected *action*. He did not need men who were satisfied just to sit down and talk about the Kingdom of God. He had work for them to do, teaching, preaching, and healing. And he wanted them to live the things they learned from him.

He expected *obedience*. He was going to send his disciples out into the country and towns and cities. He wanted them to do the kind of things he was doing for people. He must have men who would obey the instructions that he gave them.

And he wished their *love*. He knew that if they loved him more than they loved anyone else, he would have their trust, their loyalty, their learning, their action, and their obedience.

After Jesus had gone from the earth his followers became very numerous. For a while people hardly knew what to call them, and gave them many names, such as Followers of the Way, Brethren, Friends, and Saints. But finally the name that came to be used most was "Christians," because they believed in Christ and were his followers.

All the Christians as a body were called "the church." The word "church" means those who have been called out. So when Christians were referred to as "the church" it helped them to remember that every Christian was still a person who had been called out to be a follower of Christ.

And just as it was when Jesus was on earth, so also after he was gone, it was expected of all his followers that they should trust him, be loyal to him, keep on learning about him and his teaching, act in obedience to him, and love him.

Today

We need Jesus today, just as much as the people did in those days long ago. You often hear persons talking about the situation in our world, in this country, and in every country. We are eager for deliverance, just as they were then. We are sinful, just as people were then. We need him as our Deliverer, our Redeemer, our Saviour.

And he needs followers today, just as he has always needed them, in every community, whether it is in the country, or in the towns, or in the cities.

II

PROFESSION OF FAITH

Joining the Church

You have often heard people speak of "joining the church." But has anyone ever told you how a person joins the church?

Some persons become members of the church when they are born! For Presbyterians believe that the church includes not only the older people who have said they wished to become followers of Jesus, but it also includes the children of those people, if they have any children. That is one of the reasons why Presbyterians baptize babies, if the parents wish it. These babies who have been baptized are members of the church already. You could not say they are going to "join the church" when they are older, because they are already members of the church. Sometimes we say these boys and girls are "children of the covenant." Later we shall learn more about this.

But these boys and girls who were baptized when they were babies are not fully members in every way, until they themselves say they want to be. When they decide for themselves that they wish to be followers of Jesus, we should not say they are going to join the church. We should say they are going to be admitted to the Lord's Supper.

Some other boys and girls were born in homes where the parents did not wish to have the babies baptized. When these boys and girls are older and decide they wish to become followers of Christ, we often say they are going to "join the church." When they do that, of course, they also are admitted to the Lord's Supper.

Profession of Faith

There is one thing which the church asks *all* persons to do before they are received into full membership and admitted to the Lord's Supper. That one thing is to make a profession of faith in Jesus Christ. Let us see what that means.

"Profession" means telling something publicly, so that everybody who is interested can know about it. When a person makes profession of faith in Christ, he tells the members of the church that he believes in Christ as his Saviour and has decided for himself that he will be a follower of Christ.

Many boys and girls have lived in Christian homes and have known about Jesus all their lives. They have loved him and trusted him as long as they can remember. They cannot remember a time when they did not love him and trust him. They have had faith in him since they first came to know about him. But a profession of faith is one way of telling the other people of the church that we *do* have faith in Christ, and that we mean to be a follower of his as long as we live.

Some boys and girls, though, have not thought much about things of this kind when they were younger. But in the church school, or at home, or from something they read, or from the minister's sermon, or from somebody who talked with them about it, they learned something that made them begin to think about following Jesus.

And the more they think about it, the more they begin to feel as the followers of Jesus did long ago. Perhaps they say something of this kind to themselves: "I trust him as Lord and Saviour, because he died for me and I believe the things he taught are true. I want to be loyal to him as the Leader of my life. I want to keep on learning more about him, and more about the things he taught. I mean to try to do the things he taught, for I want to obey him as the one who shall tell me how to live."

If any boy or girl thinks about Jesus in that way, that *is* loving him and having faith in him.

Our Lord

When we profess faith in Christ, we take Christ to be our Lord. That means we ask him to be the Teacher and Leader of our lives. You remember that he wished to be the King of men's hearts. When we take him as our Lord, we are asking him to be the King of *our* hearts.

Our Saviour

And when we profess faith in Christ, we take him to be our Saviour. After Jesus had died and had risen from the dead, his followers began to understand, as they could not do before that time, that Jesus is not only our Leader and Teacher, but that he is our Saviour also. As long as he was with them in the body, they knew that he had lived for his followers. But now they saw more clearly that he had also died for his followers. They knew that every person is a sinner, for each of us does things that are sinful, and fails to do many things he should do. They knew that each of us needs to be forgiven by God for his sins, and that each of us needs to be kept from doing things that are sinful. They knew Jesus had died in their place, that he rose again and stood ready to deliver them from sin in their daily lives. So they spoke of Jesus as our Saviour, who died for us on the cross.

Often we say that Jesus Christ as our Saviour made atonement for us, or atoned for our sins. "Atonement" is one of many great experiences which Christians wish to understand better and better as they grow. It is so rich an experience that perhaps we shall never understand it fully as long as we live. But you can make a beginning if you will remember a time when you had a misunderstanding with a friend, and then later were reconciled or made one in spirit again. The two of you then had become "at one." Long ago our forefathers in England spoke of this as "at-one-ment," or atonement. In translating the Bible this word atonement was helpful, and Christians have used it often since, for it expresses so much of what Christ did for us.

For example, as you read and study the story of Jesus in the four Gospels you will see, again and again, how he was seeking to lead men who had misunderstood God, to love and trust the Father in heaven. This was reconciling men to God.

And the writers of the books in the New Testament constantly are reminding us of Jesus Christ our Saviour and his atonement. You might like to study a few of these passages now. Colossians 1:18-22 is speaking of Christ; what does Paul say about Christ's reconciling us? Or read Hebrews 9:13-15; what are we told that Christ is? And in I Peter 2:21-24, what are we told that Christ did for us?

So when we speak of a profession of faith, now, we are thinking of taking Jesus Christ as the Lord of our lives, and we are thinking of taking him as our Saviour.

Born Again

When it is the desire of our hearts to profess faith in Jesus Christ as Lord and Saviour, we may know that it is God's Spirit who has caused us to feel that way. Such a person has been made "a new creature," as Paul said. We often say that he has been born again, or that he has been regenerated. Many persons do not ever know *when*

27

that great change took place within, but they can know that it *has* taken place because they wish to profess their faith in Christ and live as he taught us to live. So we do not have to wait for some strange, mysterious feeling inside of us. If we desire to become followers of Christ, we can know with all certainty that he desires us to be that, and will accept us as his followers. What we need to do then is to act, and not just keep on wondering about it. And *we can act by making a profession of our faith in Christ.*

Making a Profession

In making a profession of faith, three steps are usually to be taken.

The first of these is to talk with the minister of the church, and tell him that you wish to make profession of faith as soon as he thinks it is wise for you to do so. He will be glad to talk with you about it. Before you speak with him, of course you will talk it over with your parents, or with your guardian if your parents are not living. It may be they will also wish to talk with the minister, and perhaps you could all go to see him together.

The Examination

The second step in making a profession of faith is an examination before the Session of the church. While this is called an "examination," it is not like a school examination in any way. It is just meeting and talking with a group of persons whom you probably know already. These people are called "the Session." The Session consists of the pastor of the church and the elders. Perhaps you have seen the elders serving the Lord's Supper.

When the minister knows that someone wishes to make profession of faith, he asks the Session to meet. If you are ready to make your profession, you go in to meet with them. You need not go alone, if you wish someone to go with you.

The minister usually asks you some questions. A Presbyterian minister is not required to ask exactly the same questions of everybody. If you wish, you may ask your own pastor just what questions he asks when young people come to make profession of faith.

The minister often makes the questions very simple. For example, he might say something like this, when he is talking with a person who is a child of the covenant, and has been baptized in infancy:

James, we know that you have been learning about our Lord Jesus Christ since you were very young. When you were baptized, your parents promised to rear you as a child of God. They believed in Christ, and they hoped you would have faith in him also. They hoped that as soon as you were old enough, you yourself would make your own profession of faith. You are doing that today. You are already a baptized member of the church, but now you are asking to be admitted to the Lord's Supper, and you are asking to be received into full responsibility in the church. Let me ask you these questions, and if you can do so, will you answer each one by saying, "I do."

Do you now profess your own faith in Jesus Christ?

Do you ask him to be your Lord and Saviour?

Do you promise that, with God's help, you will try to live as a follower of Jesus Christ ought to live?

Do you promise to carry your part of the responsibility of the church, by attending its worship and supporting its work as faithfully as you can?

Do you promise that you will permit yourself to be governed by the officers of the church where they have the right to govern you?

Do you promise to try to discover ways in which you can make this a better church, and help it to grow?

When the minister is talking with young persons who are still to be baptized, he may say something of this kind:

Frank, the church has taught you about our Lord Jesus Christ, and has sought to help you understand what it means to become a Christian and live as a Christian. You have made up your own mind that you wish to be a follower of Jesus. You have come to make your own profession of faith in Jesus Christ, asking that we baptize you and receive you into the membership of the church. Let me ask you these questions, and if you can do so, will you answer each one by saying, "I do."

The questions the minister then asks Frank will probably be the same as those which he asked James.

Frank, and any others who have not been baptized previously, may be baptized during the meeting of the Session, or before the congregation.

Public Reception

The third step is taken when the persons who have made profession of faith are publicly received as members. This is done in different ways.

In some churches the minister asks those who have just made profession of faith to stand before the congregation, and he speaks briefly to welcome them.

In some other churches the service is more elaborate. A few questions like those asked in the examination are asked again before the congregation. All the persons professing faith in Jesus Christ make the responses together.

And sometimes those who have not yet been baptized are baptized before the congregation.

If you do not know how all this is done in your own church, you may get the information from your minister.

III

THE CREED

The Importance of Beliefs

ONE day recently, in the Far East, a prisoner was brought from jail, and stood before the police. The first question seemed a strange thing for the police to ask a prisoner. "What do you believe about God?" they wanted to know. They questioned him about it for hours, for the man was a Christian, and the police were determined to find out whether he was more loyal to God than he was to the king of that country.

All over the world today many Christians are in the same position as that man. Of course they are not all prisoners, but they are finding it is necessary to decide, "Who shall be the final ruler of my life? Shall it be God, or shall it be the government?" They are loyal to their government, and wish to obey it. They love their country, for it is home. But does a time ever come when a Christian cannot obey both God and government? Many Christians, in almost every country, are having to decide that question. And their answer *depends upon what they believe*.

Nearly any day you have to decide some important question about what you will do. You ask, "Is this right, or is it wrong?" Sometimes others can help you decide, but often you must decide in your own heart, alone. And the answer *depends upon what you believe*.

At this time in your life you are seeking to decide what kind of person you will be, what things you will live for, what rules you will choose to govern yourself, what kind of persons you will seek for your closest friends, and many, many questions of that sort. The answers you give *depend on what you believe*. For if you believe Jesus is worthy to be the Ruler of your life, you will seek to know what he wishes his followers to be, and you will try to obey his will.

The more you think about it, the more importance you will see there is in the things you believe. But Protestant churches do not say to people, "Here are the things you must believe." Instead, they say, "Here is what our church believes. We invite you to study it. We hope you will make it your own, so that you can say, 'I believe this.' "

And you are invited today to study some of the great Christian beliefs.

"I Believe"

The people who were the earliest followers of Jesus were enthusiastic about him. They believed in him.

But that was not all. They believed certain things about him. For example, they believed he was the Messiah, the Deliverer whom the Jews were expecting. They believed he was "the Lord"; that meant he was the Ruler, the King, the Master. It was the same word they often used when they spoke of God. They believed he was the Son of God. They believed he had suffered and died on the cross for them. They believed he had risen again from the dead. And they believed he would come to the world again.

But many other persons had quite different beliefs about Jesus. Some thought he was a good man, but that he certainly was not the Son of God. Others thought he certainly was the Son of God, but that he was not really a man, that he only looked and acted like one. And there were many other beliefs about him, some of them very strange.

The Christians were troubled by such beliefs about Jesus. They knew that people who thought of Jesus in these ways did not understand him, and could not know his power in their lives.

So the older Christians took the converts and taught them about Jesus. A convert was a person who had never been a Christian, but had decided to become one. And when a convert had been taught about Jesus and about the Christian beliefs and about how a Christian should live, the minister or priest began to ask him, "What do you believe?"

The things a person said he believed were called his confession, or his confession of faith. A confession of faith is also called a "creed," for the word *credo* in Latin means, "I believe."

Usually a convert made his confession of faith when he was baptized. It was a custom in some churches for the priest to ask, "Dost thou believe in God the Father Almighty?" The candidate for baptism would reply, "I believe." The priest then baptized him.

The priest then asked, "Dost thou believe in Christ Jesus, the Son of God, who was born of the Holy Ghost of the Virgin Mary, and was crucified under Pontius Pilate, and was dead and buried, and rose again the third day, alive from the dead, and ascended into heaven, and sat at the right hand of the Father, and will come to judge the quick and the dead?" The candidate replied, "I believe." And he was baptized a second time.

The priest asked a third question: "Dost thou believe in Holy Ghost, and the Holy Church, and the resurrection of the flesh?" The candidate answered, "I believe." And he was baptized a third time.

The Apostles' Creed

There were many creeds, almost alike, but the one that is best known now is called "The Apostles' Creed." It is the confession of faith which many thousands, and probably many millions, of persons have said at the time when they were baptized or at the time when they were admitted to the Lord's Supper.

If you do not know it, surely you will wish to memorize it. And whenever you say it, it is well to think of two kinds of things. First, of course, you will always want to think of the things you are saying. But in the back of your mind you can also think of the countless number of other Christians, white, and black, and yellow, and brown people, who have used this as their confession. The Apostles' Creed is this:

I believe in God the Father Almighty, Maker of heaven and earth; and in Jesus Christ his only Son our Lord; who was conceived by the Holy Ghost; born of the Virgin Mary; suffered under Pontius Pilate; was crucified, dead, and buried; he descended into hell; the third day he rose again from the dead; he ascended into heaven; and sitteth on the right hand of God the Father Almighty; from thence he shall come to judge the quick and the dead. I believe in the Holy Ghost; the holy catholic church; the communion of saints; the forgiveness of sins; the resurrection of the body; and the life everlasting. Amen.

The Presbyterian Creed

Most denominations have creeds. These creeds usually take up such matters as are mentioned in the Apostles' Creed, and other things as well, and seek to explain them more thoroughly.

The Presbyterians have their creed. It is found in what we call our Constitution. That Constitution has four parts: The Confession of Faith, the Larger Catechism, the Shorter Catechism, and the Book of Church

Order. Our creed as Presbyterians consists of the first three parts of our Constitution, that is, the Confession of Faith, the Larger Catechism, and the Shorter Catechism. Each of these says about the same things, but says them in different ways, and for a different purpose. The Confession of Faith is the most complete and thorough part of our creed. The Shorter Catechism is the briefest part of the Presbyterian creed.

Growing in Our Beliefs

Great Christian men and women have toiled in order to express the Christian beliefs more and more accurately. Just as the scientists have labored so that we may know God's world better, so these persons whom we call students of theology have toiled so that we might understand God's Word better.

Young Christians owe it to God, to the church, and to themselves, to determine, "I do want to know more and more of the things that Christians believe."

If young Christians make that resolve, and really carry it out, they become stronger and more intelligent Christians.

And this is one of the surest ways of keeping intelligent liberty in our religion and in our government. Many countries have lost that liberty, in their religion and in their government. We can gratefully say we still have it. We must be sure that we use it right. It may be that God has entrusted it to us so we can help him save it for the world.

One of the principal reasons why we still have liberty is that the men and women who went before us did just what the church is inviting its boys and girls to do now, and that is to know what the Christian beliefs are, to study them more earnestly than we study anything else, and to keep on growing in our understanding and our use of the Christian faith.

The minister can tell you of ways you can begin now. Perhaps you would like to discuss these in the class, and determine to make the start.

IV
BAPTISM

Initiation

THE Christian church is sometimes called a society. Some societies require you to be initiated when you join. The church has an initiation, too. But the initiation into the church is not secret, for the church wishes everyone to know when a new member is initiated. And the initiation into the church is not a funny one, as some initiations are, for *baptism* is the initiation into the Christian church, and when you see such a service you feel quiet and thankful.

When a person is initiated into a society, often the initiation has a meaning which you might not think of unless somebody told you what it was. In one society a large circle was painted on the floor, and a heart was painted in the middle of the circle. During the initiation, the members of the society stood on the circle, and the new member stood on the heart while he was making his pledge. That meant that the persons who were already members of the society were saying to the new member, "We are taking you into our circle and into our hearts." But they did not ever say that in words. They only said it by *acting it out*.

When we act out a meaning, we call the action a *symbol*. And baptism is a symbol, for it has a meaning which is acted out. When the minister baptizes a person, that is one way of telling us that things of great importance are taking place in the life of the person who is being initiated into the church. We shall see what some of these things are.

God's Spirit

Some societies will not receive you into membership until you prove that you "have the spirit" of that society. They want you to show that spirit wherever you go, and live it whatever you do.

The Bible and Christian people often speak of the spirit of Christ in that way. If we have his spirit, we will think, and feel, and act, as he did. For example, we will be considerate of other people, truthful, kind to little children, and do what we know is right even when it is unpopular. You might like to read Romans 8:15, and II Timothy 1:7. You will see that Paul was thinking of a spirit in the Christian that is like the character or spirit of Christ.

Sometimes we also speak of God's character or spirit in the same way. In I John 4:1-6 you can see that John was thinking of a spirit in the Christian which is like the character or spirit of God.

But Christ's Spirit, or God's Spirit, means more than that. It means a person, just as truly as God is a person and Jesus is a person. So Christians speak of the Holy Spirit, or the Holy Ghost, for *ghost* is an old word meaning *spirit*. The Holy Spirit is a person who does God's work in the world and in our lives. If we have a spirit or character that is at all like the character of Christ, we do so because God has sent his Holy Spirit into our hearts. It was God's Spirit who caused us to be that way.

Do you remember what you have seen taking place when the minister baptizes a person? He puts water on the head of that person, saying, "I baptize thee into the name of the Father, and of the Son, and of the Holy Spirit. Amen." And *the water coming upon the person is a symbol of God's Holy Spirit coming into that person's life.*

We may think, now, of four other things that baptism means. These are things that God does for us, or makes possible for us, when his Spirit comes to us.

Our Cleansing

We use water to make our bodies clean. Our hearts need to be made clean just as truly as our bodies do. And the water coming upon the body is a symbol to remind us that God's Spirit cleanses our hearts.

When our heart is cleansed of sin, we call that "regeneration," which means being born again. We have a different spirit because God's Spirit has come into our hearts, changing us. In Titus 3:5 (A. S. V.) Paul calls this "the washing of regeneration and renewing of the Holy Spirit." *Baptism is a symbol of God's Holy Spirit cleansing the person's heart, and changing his spirit.*

Our Ingrafting

In the woods, native grapevines often grow wild. Sometimes a gardener has another kind of grape in his orchard, which he likes because the taste is so fine. But perhaps the grape in the orchard has a weak vine, and cannot yield many grapes. So the gardener may take a piece of the grapevine from his orchard and graft it on the native vine. The piece of vine from the orchard now begins to grow from the sap of the native vine, because now it has powerful roots of the wild vine to feed it.

In Romans 11:17-19 Paul was writing about persons who believed in Christ, and he said they were grafted into Christ. They were so closely united to Christ that they received their strength from him, and grew as he wished them to grow.

This symbol gives us one of the meanings of baptism, that is, that we are "ingrafted into Christ." *The person being baptized is being initiated into the society of people who are united to Christ.*

The Covenant

When people make a promise to each other, and wish it to be so impressive they will never forget it, they sometimes make a covenant. When a man and woman marry, they promise to be faithful to each other always; that is a covenant. When a king and his people make pledges to each other, that, too, is a covenant.

And God has made a covenant, called the covenant of grace. He has promised eternal life to all who believe in Jesus Christ. Eternal life means that our soul shall live and grow always, in God's care and keeping. We do not have to wait until we die to have eternal life. It begins as soon as we begin to have faith in Christ, and continues forever.

Baptism means that God is promising eternal life to the person who is being baptized, if he has faith in Christ. The meaning which the minister is acting out is that *God is making a pledge, and God will keep his promise.* You remember that when one makes profession of faith, he makes a pledge that he will be faithful to Christ and his church. Baptism is a way of telling us that whenever we make our pledge to Christ, *God* is also making *his* pledge to us.

Our Engagement

When a man and a woman announce their engagement, they wish everyone to know that they are loyal to each other. Baptism has a meaning similar to that, too, for it is a symbol of "our engagement to be the Lord's." We have pledged our faith to Christ, and *now we are his, to be loyal to him as long as life shall last.* We cannot

43

wear a ring to show it, but our baptism is a "sign and seal" that it is so.

The Baptism of Little Children

The church includes in its membership those who have made their profession of faith, and it also includes their children. For God's promises are not only made to those who are old enough to have faith in Christ. Those promises are also made to their children. So the children of Christian parents are called the "children of the covenant."

And these children of the covenant may be baptized when they are infants. When they are that small they are not old enough to have faith in Christ, themselves. But their parents do have that faith. Do you remember seeing a little child baptized? And do you remember that the *parents* answered the minister's questions? They promise that they will live with him as a Christian, teach him the Christian religion while he is growing, and help him so that he, too, may come to have faith in Christ. And Christian parents believe that *God begins to keep his promise to give eternal life, even when a child is very small, if that child is in a truly Christian home.*

So when a child is baptized, in many ways the meaning of the baptism is just the same as it is when an older person is baptized. We believe God's Spirit is coming into the life of this child of a Christian home. We believe that he already belongs in the society of persons who are "in-

44

grafted into Christ." We believe that God makes his pledge of cleansing and of eternal life to this child of the covenant, and that he is "engaged to be the Lord's."

But the baptism of a child is different from that of an older person, in three ways. One is that the infant of Christian parents is not being *initiated* as a member; he is being *recognized* as a member of the church.

Another difference is that the parents make the pledge, since a little child is too young to make his own pledge yet. If parents do not keep that pledge, and if the church or someone else does not teach the child as he grows, God cannot keep *his* pledge, because the child then will not know about God and Christ. But if they keep their pledge carefully, the child will grow up as a Christian, and will never remember any time when he was not a Christian.

Still another difference is that a little child who has been baptized does not become fully a member of the church in every way until he makes his own profession of faith. When he pledges his own loyalty to Christ and the church, he is admitted to the Lord's Supper.

V

THE LORD'S SUPPER

Your First Communion

SOME of you are soon to take your first Communion. The Communion is the time when we have the Lord's Supper. From the time when you first began going to church, you have often seen the congregation at the Lord's Supper. Christians think of this as one of the most precious of all times. When you have made your own profession of faith, you, too, will partake of the Lord's Supper. Your family and friends, who have already confessed Christ, will partake with you in a Communion which you probably will remember always.

You will wish to know how we came to observe the Lord's Supper, what it means to us, and how we should partake of it. Let us think about it now.

The Last Supper

The celebration of the Lord's Supper comes to us from the days of our Lord Jesus. The Jewish people had the beautiful custom of observing the Passover. That was a special meal they ate together as a family, once a year. They looked forward to it for weeks, and when the time came they ate it reverently and joyfully.

For it recalled the memory of a great deliverance which God had given them in Egypt, long before.

On the night before he was betrayed, Jesus sat down with his little company of disciples, at this ancient meal. They were troubled, for they knew danger was ahead, but they did not understand how great the danger was.

But Jesus knew that death was soon to come to him. He wished his disciples, and all Christians of later years, to have one thing that would bind them together forever. He determined that his death should be that one thing. When they thought of his death, he wished them never to think he had been defeated, for he was not defeated. He wished them never to think he had gone away, for he had not. He wished them to be thankful because he had been willing to die for them, for as he himself said, he laid down his life for his own. He wished them to rejoice because he had died, instead of being full of sorrow over it. He wished his death to draw their hearts together more and more closely until they would feel as if they all had but one heart, and that he was always in that heart.

So while they were eating, at the last supper which Jesus had with his disciples, he took some of the bread, blessed it, broke it, and gave it to them. As he gave them the bread, he said, "This is my body, which is broken for you: this do in remembrance of me."

Then he took a cup of wine, and said, "This cup is the

new covenant in my blood: this do, as often as ye drink it, in remembrance of me."

Today

In our churches today we still celebrate that Supper, as Jesus commanded his disciples to do.

The minister blesses the bread, breaks it, hands it to the elders, and they pass it to the congregation. Then the minister takes wine, or perhaps grape juice, often in individual cups, hands it to the elders, and they pass that to the congregation.

The only persons who may partake of the bread and wine are those who have professed faith in Christ and have been received into full membership in a church. But it does not have to be a Presbyterian church. If any of your friends or family are members of other Christian churches and wish to be with you at the Communion, they may do so.

When the bread is passed, we take one small piece. When the wine is passed, we take one of the individual cups. If a large cup is used, each person takes one tiny sip.

After we have taken the bread, and again after we have taken the wine, we sit very quietly so we can think and pray. Talking, or laughing, or turning to watch other people, is always poor manners after church has begun, but especially so at the Communion. After they have taken the bread or the wine, many persons like to close their eyes so their hearts can be quieter. But whether we do just that or not, we do wish to think and pray.

And perhaps you would like to know some of the things that Christian people think about and pray about, at the Communion. That will help us to understand better what the Communion means. And it is suitable to think of things such as these, either when we are preparing our hearts for the Communion, or when we are partaking of it.

Remembering Jesus

When Jesus gave the bread, and again when he gave the wine, he said, "This do in remembrance of me."

So the Lord's Supper is a time for remembering Jesus, and thinking of him. At other times when we remember Jesus, perhaps we think of some of the many things he said, or did. But at the Communion, we especially remember that he died for us. For the bread that is broken is a symbol of his body that was broken on the cross for us. And the wine poured out into the cup is a symbol of his blood, his very life, given for us.

At the Communion, and especially when we are preparing for it, it is right for us to confess to God the wrong, sinful things we have done. Perhaps we shall say, "I did this mean thing. I said that spiteful thing. I hurt someone in his heart. I am very sorry now, Lord.

I repent of my sins. Help me not to do these wrong things again." But when we have confessed our sins, it is best not to keep on thinking about them. Just tell God, and ask his forgiveness. Then again remember Jesus.

Many Christians say something like this in their hearts during the Communion, when they are thinking about Jesus; they say it quietly, so only God hears it; "That dear, strong Body was broken *for me*. His blood, his life itself, was given *for me*. He died for *my* sins. I am one of that great company, 'the church of the Lord which he purchased with his own blood.' "

And often that makes our hearts feel like singing with thankfulness and joy. For at the Communion, when we think of Jesus' death, it is not a time of sadness. It is a time for thanksgiving.

Communion with Christ

Jesus wished his followers to feel that his Spirit is always with us. Baptism, you recall, is a symbol reminding us that the Spirit has come into our lives. And the Lord's Supper is especially a time when we know that his Spirit *is* with us, now.

For the Lord's Supper helps us to have communion with Christ. Communion means sharing. Fellowship means the same thing. When we have friendship, or fellowship, with a friend whom we can see, we can share life with that friend because we can see him and talk with him. We cannot see Jesus, and it is easy to forget how near his Spirit is. But the Lord's Supper brings him to our minds again. It helps us to remember how much he shared with us. And it invites us to share still more of our life with him.

And when the congregation is taking the Communion, often you feel something that is different from other times. Everyone is quiet and still, but it is not a lonesome stillness. Neither is it like the stillness when we are tired and sleepy. It is more like the time when we are waiting for a friend to speak to us. Or often it is like the time when we are with some very dear friend, not talking for a little while, but enjoying just being together. For at the Lord's Supper, we are communing with Christ.

Communion with Other Christians

At the Lord's Supper we not only remember Jesus and have communion with him, but we also share with other Christians in their communion with Christ.

In old churches long ago they used to have little tablets, and each tablet had on it the name of some person who was a member of that church. When a person died, they left his tablet right where it had always been, for he was still a member of the church. He had gone from their sight, but he was always a part of the church. The names of the living and the dead

IDLEWILD PRESBYTERIAN CHURCH
1750 UNION AVENUE
MEMPHIS 4, TENN

were read at the Communion. So when the people came to the church they felt they were still in the company of all who had ever worshipped there.

We do not have that custom now, but we do have the same thought. The church is more than the people whom we see together on Sunday. It includes men, and women, and children, from every country, of every century.

And at the Communion, often we feel all tingling with the thought of that great host of people, marching onward through life, long ago, and now, and still to come. For each one of us who is a Christian, whether young or old, is part of this mighty host, stronger than any society the world has ever seen or will ever see. It is the Church of the Living God!

VI

DECISION

Making Choices

JANET had an allowance. She was saving so she could get a watch. Every day she thought of things she would like to buy, but she knew that if she spent all her money on candy and shows, she would have none left for the watch. Each day she had to decide what she wanted most.

Robert was planning to be a doctor. He was in Junior High School, where he could select the courses he wanted to take. One semester he had to decide between Latin and Band. If he took Band, he would have more fun while he was in Junior High. But a doctor told Robert that if he took Latin it would always help him in understanding the things he would study as a doctor. He had to decide which he wanted most.

Everyone has to make choices, constantly. If we are careless, thinking we'll just take today's fun and forget tomorrow, we stay like children who have good times now but cannot see any further, and need someone else to make decisions for them. But if we make choices wisely, we grow, and can be trusted with still more important decisions.

In Our Religion

In our religion there are many choices we need to make as we cease being children. When we were small, many of the choices were made for us. But someone else cannot keep on making these choices for us. As we grow older, we must make the choices ourselves.

The greatest choice we have to make is deciding whether we shall make profession of faith in Jesus Christ. For in taking Jesus as Lord and Saviour, we are deciding who shall govern our hearts and our living, now and always. We are deciding who shall be our Leader, showing and telling us what the best kind of life is. He "governs our hearts" when *we* want to do what *he* wants us to do. No one else can make a choice of that kind for us. If it is to be made, we must make it ourselves.

The Invitation

In our earlier lessons we have studied what it means to be a follower of Jesus, to profess faith in him, to be baptized, and to be admitted to the Lord's Supper.

Today, each member of the class is invited to decide in his own heart, "*I* will make *my* profession of faith in Jesus Christ."

In some of our other lessons we learned about certain outward things we do when we make profession of faith. We go before the Session and are asked a few simple questions, we are publicly received into the full membership of the church, and we are admitted to the Lord's Supper.

But today, when we are invited to make our profession of faith, each one should ask himself, "What is it I am deciding, when I make a profession of faith?"

A Follower of Jesus

When we make a profession of faith in Jesus Christ, there are two things, especially, that we are deciding. The first is, *"I decide to be a follower of Jesus."*

Perhaps we have already been trying to be that, for a long time. Since we were very small, perhaps we have been trying to live as he taught us to live. Or, it may be we have only recently begun to think about it. But no matter how long ago or how recently we began, if we make a profession of faith in Christ, that means we are now deciding to let everyone know who our Leader is. Other people helped us decide many things when we were younger, but now we are choosing for ourselves, openly, so everybody may know it.

When we are thinking about this decision to be a follower of Jesus always, there are some things we may say in our own hearts, if we wish, to help us know better what it means when we decide to be a follower of Jesus.

One would be to say, inwardly as a prayer, "I take Christ as my Lord." Then we might try to think what that means. If we wish, we could say in our hearts, as a prayer, "He is my Lord. When I say that, I mean he is to be my Leader, the Ruler of my life. I commit myself to him, I turn myself over to him so that I may obey him. When I have choices to make in my daily living, I shall try to choose what he would want me to choose."

Another thing one might say, inwardly as a prayer, is this: "I accept Christ as my Saviour." Then we might try to think what that, too, means. We might say in our hearts, as a prayer, "I need a Saviour every day. Many times I have done things that were wrong, sinful. Many times I have needed to be forgiven. I shall need to be forgiven many times in the future. I ask to be forgiven for every wrong thing, every sin, I have done, and I know that God forgives those who ask sincerely to be forgiven. Always in the future I shall seek to remember that Christ died for me and that God, for Christ's sake, forgives those who ask to be forgiven. I shall try to remember, and never forget, that God forgives whenever I need to be forgiven. And I not only ask him to forgive, but I ask him to help me, every day, to do the things I ought to do and turn away from the things I ought not to do."

A Member of the Church

When we make a profession of faith in Christ, the first choice we are making is, "I decide to be a follower of Jesus Christ." And the other choice we are making is, *"I decide to be a member of the church of Jesus Christ."*

Perhaps we were children of the covenant, born as

members of the church. If so, that was a great privilege, one of the greatest we shall ever have. But that does not mean there is nothing left for us to decide for ourselves. Indeed, being born in the church makes it all the more necessary that we shall come to a time when we say, "I want this privilege of church membership, not just because it came to me when I was born, but because I love it myself and choose it now for myself."

Or, if we knew very little about the church until recently, perhaps now we have come to understand better how much it means, and we say, "I want to be a member."

When we say, "I decide to be a member of the church of Jesus Christ," we are choosing our side in the great game of life. The world is like a vast game in which there are many teams, each team trying to win the victory for its cause and its leader.

And deciding to be a member of the church of Jesus Christ is a way of saying, "I enlist with Christ and his church." If we wish to think what that means, we might say something like this, inwardly, as a prayer: "O God, I see so many teams trying to win the victory in the world, some by force, some by cruelty, some by deceit, some by kindness. I want to be on the side of those who are trying to live in kindliness with other people, who are seeking to win the game not by hatred but by love. I want to be on the side of Jesus Christ. I want to do my part as a member of his church."

My Decision

We need Jesus as our Lord and Saviour, and he needs us as members of his church. Today we have thought carefully about the decision to make profession of our faith in him, and we have thought of what that decision means.

It may be that our decision is already reached in our hearts. If it is, we shall want to let the minister know, so plans can be made for the day when we shall actually make that profession.

But before we speak to him about our decision, we may read this prayer to see what is said in it, and then after it has been read each one who feels he can do so will be asked to read it silently as his own prayer of decision.

"Our Father, help me to decide right today. I have one life to live. It is precious to me, and I know it is even more precious to thee than it can be to me, because Christ died for me. I want my life to be the best life possible. I want it to count, wherever I live it. And now, of my own free will, and gladly, I turn my life over to thee. I decide to be a follower of Jesus Christ as long as I live. I take him as my Saviour, and as the Lord of my life. I decide, of my own choice, to be a member of the church. I ask thee to help me to be a worthy follower of Christ, a worthy member of the church, to the end of my life here. I entrust my life to thee, not only now, but forever. In the name of Jesus Christ our Lord and Saviour. Amen."

Part Two

FOR HOME READING

These chapters are for home reading and study, after you have completed the study of the first six chapters in class. In the class we studied about becoming a Christian. These next chapters are meant to help you in growing as a Christian. If you will, you may study these chapters carefully at home, perhaps taking one a day, or one a week.

I

IN TRAINING

In Training

THE school at Jackson was proud of having the best foot-ball team of its class in the state. Jim Walton wanted to make that team. He wanted it so much that he practiced as hard as he could, worked his best to keep his school record up, and kept training perfectly. When at last the coach announced the first team, to play against the Speers School, Jim was on it.

Jim was so happy he could hardly sleep. When the Jackson-Speers game was played, Jackson won. Jim had played magnificently, making a long run which broke a tie in the score. It was a great day in Jim's life.

The big game of the season was with the Albany team. Everybody was saying, "Jim, we're counting on you to win that game." It began to go to his head. Thinking he was so fast in the field no one could catch him, he began to break training on the sly. When the big game came, it was very close, and again there was a tie in the last quarter. In the last few minutes the ball was passed to Jim, and he started for another long run. But he had broken training too often, and he was slow that day. He was caught, lost the ball, an Albany man gained possession of it, made a touchdown, and Jackson lost the game.

Keeping Training

If we stay in training in any form of athletics or sports, we are better able to keep growing in our skill. We get more fun out of the game, and our team is more likely to be strong, with a better chance to win.

And something very like that is true in many other places besides athletics and sports. If we wish to grow, and if we wish to help our team instead of being a handicap, we must obey the rules, especially when we are being trusted and nobody is watching to see how well we keep them.

In the Church

Somewhat the same kind of thing is true when one becomes a responsible member of the church. He needs to keep up his training so that he can steadily become a better member of his church.

If we are received into the full membership of the church, and then begin on the sly to break the rules that were meant to help us grow and make the church stronger, by and by the people of our church will begin to wonder whether we are playing fair. They will think, "What's the matter with Jim? He started out as a good member, but he's no help to us now as he has grown older. He is still like a child, needing somebody to do everything for him, and not able to carry his own part yet."

But if we stay in training, even when nobody is watching, the result is very different. People begin to say, "That is the kind of boy or girl you can count on." They begin to trust that sort of person with more and more responsibility in the church and in the community. And such a person is not only able to carry his own part, but is a help to "his team"—his church—because he is growing.

We are to think together how a young Christian may continue to grow after he has made a profession of faith in Christ and been admitted to full responsibility in the church.

The First Rule

The first secret of a young Christian's growth is that he makes the rule *for himself* that he will stay in training as a Christian.

The young Christian has taken Christ as his Lord. As you remember, that means that Christ is now our first Leader, our Master. And we may determine in our hearts, if we will, something of this kind.

"I shall play fair with my Leader, Christ, the very best I know how. I have trusted him, and now he is trusting me. I have asked him to be my Saviour, because he lived and died for me. I will not back down, now, when he asks me to do something for him. I have asked him to be my Lord, my Leader, the Ruler of my heart. And now I'm going to play fair with him, right from the start, by staying in training as a Christian, so that I may grow to be of more and more value to my Lord and my church."

The Kingdom That No One Sees

Jesus often spoke of "the kingdom of God," and when we understand what he meant by that, perhaps we can understand better why a Christian will *want* to stay in training and will *want* to do the kind of things that bring growth.

In Matthew 16:13-19 there is a story that you may read to help you understand what Jesus meant by the Kingdom of God.

This story tells of Jesus and his disciples who were talking one day, when Jesus asked, "Who do people say I am?" They told him some of the things people were saying. Then Jesus asked, "Whom say ye that I am?" Peter had been coming to know Jesus better and better, for months. And that day Peter replied, "Thou art the Christ, the Son of the living God."

This is called "Peter's confession." You will remember that we studied, in the class, about a confession of faith, when we tell others what we believe. And this was like a profession of faith, also, because Peter expressed his faith in Jesus as the Christ, or Messiah, whom the Jews had been expecting.

When Peter had professed his faith in Jesus as the Christ, Jesus spoke to Peter about two things: the church, and the Kingdom of God. And we want to see what the difference is between the church and the Kingdom of God.

When we make profession of faith in Christ, we enlist with Christ as our Leader, our Lord and Saviour. And we become fully responsible members of the church.

The church that we enter is something that people can see and know about, because everybody who wishes can learn who the members are and can see them.

But when we profess faith in Christ we also enter into something that nobody can see in the same way they can see the church as a group of people. We enter what Jesus called the Kingdom of God.

The Kingdom of God does not mean a country that God rules over. It means the condition of our hearts when we really and truly allow God to be the King of our hearts and to rule our lives. We are in the Kingdom of God when God is really our King.

Perhaps we can see the difference between being in the church and being in the Kingdom of God, if we think again about Jim Walton who played on the Jackson team. Jim was a member of the team, all right; that was like being a member of a church, because his name was on the list. But Jim was not really and truly controlled by the spirit of the team. That was a little bit like being in the church, but not in the Kingdom of God—for one can be a member of the church and yet not allow God really to rule his life.

Going Back Into Training

But you will be glad to know that when Jim saw what a mess he had made of the big game, he went into honest training which he would never again break, even on the sly. He made the team again the next year, and when the Jackson-Albany game came, he helped his team to win. And he did it because the spirit of the team had gotten hold of his heart and made him want to play for the team and for the school, not just for himself. And that is a little bit like permitting God to control our hearts, and to govern the way we live.

Jim had a chance to try again. And Peter had a chance to try again, too, after that day when he professed his faith in Jesus. Peter had become a disciple, a follower and friend of Jesus. But one day, near the time of the Crucifixion, when Jesus needed Peter very much, Peter failed miserably. And that was just after Peter had been at the Last Supper with Jesus, too. You might like to read about it in Mark 14, verses 26-31, and verses 65-72.

Yet after Jesus had risen from the dead, Jesus and Peter talked together as friends still. You may read that story in John 21:15-19.

Peter had broken training as a follower of Jesus, but he loved Jesus still. And when they talked together, Peter knew that Jesus trusted him still. That helped Peter to know as he had never known before, what a Leader he had in Jesus.

Desiring to Grow

When we professed our faith in Jesus Christ, just as Peter did, so we also became followers of the greatest Leader the world has ever known. But we cannot remain satisfied with just knowing that now at last we are fully members of his church. We wish to grow as Christians, so that we may continue to play fair with our Leader, our Lord.

We are to study ways by which we may grow as Christians. But now the chief thing we may remember is that our membership in the church *can* grow steadily to be a richer experience to us and a more helpful thing to others if we, in our hearts, really and truly want God to be the King of our lives. Then we shall *want* to stay in training as Christians.

II

OUR FATHER'S WORD

A Father's Diary

JACK REDMON could not remember ever seeing his father, for Mr. Redmon had died when Jack was only a few weeks old. Mrs. Redmon had told Jack many a story about his father, and Jack listened eagerly to every one of them. Each time he would think, "Oh, I wish I could have known him, myself."

One day, looking among some old papers, Jack found a diary kept by Mr. Redmon up until a few days before his death. How Jack and his mother drank in every word of it! But the thing in the diary that Jack loved most of all was an entry made a few days after Jack was born. This was what his father had written:

A son was born to us one week ago. How I love that little boy! What plans Jane and I are making, already, for him! And what a pal I mean to be to that boy!

When Jack read that, he thought for a long time, then he said to his mother, "Mother, I knew the things that father did, because you've told me about him, and I always loved him for those things. But now *I know just what he thought about me,* and I love him more than ever."

Our Father's Book

We live in a vast world, and this is only one of many worlds which make up the universe. The one who made our entire universe, and governs it, is God. He is its only Ruler, its King. But he is also our Father, as well as our King.

And in one way we are like Jack Redmon. We have a book in which we can read what God our Father thinks and feels about us, his children. That book is the Bible.

In many ways, of course, the Bible is altogether different from Jack's father's diary. Our Father in heaven is a living Father, and in another chapter we shall see that we can have a friendship in our hearts with this living Father. Our Father's Book is the Book of a living Father.

But the Bible helps us, as no other book does, to know what the mind of our Father is toward us. And it tells us, as no other book does, what God wishes us to do. For God made known to the men who wrote the Bible the truth which they wrote. When we speak of that, we say that God revealed his truth to them. And he guided them while they wrote; when we speak of that, we say God inspired them.

You might read, now, one of the things said about the Scriptures in the Bible itself. Read II Timothy 3:14-17.

Psalm 119, verses 9-16, is part of a poem written by a man who loved the Word of our Father, and who wished others to love it also. You may read it.

So our Church teaches us that all the books of the Bible "are given by inspiration of God, to be the rule of faith and life."[1] And our Shorter Catechism tells us, "The word of God, which is contained in the Scriptures of the Old and New Testaments, is the only rule to direct us how we may glorify and enjoy him."[2]

A Growing Use of the Bible

Since the Bible is our Father's Book, the growing Christian wishes to know the Bible better and better as time goes on. For in knowing our Father's Book better, we come to know our Father himself better. And the more we know him, the more we feel as Jack did—"I know better, now, what he thinks about me, and I love him all the more."

You might read the following passages, and after each one you might ask yourself, *"How* does the Bible help a Christian to grow?"—Psalm 119:9; 119:11; 119:104; 119:129, 130; Acts 1:1-3 ("the former treatise" means the Gospel of Luke); II Timothy 3:16.

As we cease to be children in age and come to be older, we should grow in our use of the Bible as we expect and try to grow in other ways. This is one of the ways we may keep in training as Christians after we have professed faith in Christ and become responsible members of the church.

1 *Westminster Confession of Faith,* Chapter I, Section 2.
2 *Shorter Catechism,* Answer to Question 2.

There are many ways we can grow in our use of the Bible as we pass beyond childhood. For example, when we were children we knew some parts of the Bible mostly because other people read them to us or told us about them. But as we become able to read more widely for ourselves, we should make the Bible one of the books which *we read for ourselves.*

When we were children, we needed to have older people to explain the hard words in the Bible for us. That may have caused us to think that the Bible is a very hard book to read. But as our vocabulary grows, we find that the Bible is *not* a hard book to read. Of course we shall meet new words, but we do that in all kinds of reading. And some parts of the Bible are not easy to understand completely, even for older people. But if a person of your age seriously tries reading the Bible for himself, regularly, he will find it is easier to read than many things we have read in school. And he will find that if he keeps on reading the Bible regularly, *he will grow in his ability to understand it.*

Getting Better Acquainted

As we read the Bible for ourselves, we might like to try different ways of reading, so as to get better acquainted with our Father's Word.

One way is to turn to some part of the Bible which we already know well and love, such as Psalm 23, and the Christmas story in Luke 2:1-20. What are some of *your* favorites? Usually we like to do this kind of reading quite slowly. No matter how many times we may have read it before, if we read carefully and think closely about what we are reading, we are likely to find something new each time. We should not hesitate to go back and read again the parts we love best, for the more we use them, the more they mean to us.

Another way is to take an entire book of the Bible and read that book through. Usually we like to do this kind of reading rapidly, so that we may get the story or the line of thought. In this manner we can read several chapters in a short time. The Gospel according to Luke would be a good book to read in this way. Then we might go next to the book of Acts. It was written by the same man, Luke, and tells the story of the early Christian church after Jesus' resurrection.

A third way is to do exploring reading; that is, to read parts of the Bible one does not know very well, or perhaps has never read. For unless a young person does some exploring in the Bible, much of it will remain unknown to him.

For example, we might explore the book of Psalms. Perhaps it is best to read the Psalms slowly, remembering that this is the Songbook of the Bible and that the Psalms are Jewish poems and songs.

Or we might explore some of the short stories of the Bible, such as the book of Ruth, or Esther, or Jonah. These may be read rapidly. When we want a longer story we might read Genesis, rapidly, skipping the lists of hard names, and reading just the story.

Many, of course, will go exploring in still other parts of the Bible. These are only samples.

Any boy or girl, beginning to read the Bible for himself, will find words and thoughts he does not understand. Often the dictionary will tell the meaning; or some older person who knows the Bible well is glad to help by explanations, if asked. And the church school is constantly helping us to get better acquainted with parts of the Bible that may be new to us now.

But a growing Christian keeps on using the Bible. Each year that he does this, he is better able to understand it, and to use it in his own living.

Keeping a Center

And a growing Christian is likely to keep some part of the Bible as a center, when he reads the Bible and thinks about it. For the Christian, that center is Jesus. The parts of the Bible which help us to know Jesus better are the parts that many Christians find most helpful. The Gospels do that, and all the other books of the New Testament do. The books of Matthew, Mark, Luke, and John are called the Gospels because they tell the Good News of Jesus.

A boy or girl who wishes to grow as a Christian may keep on exploring the other books of the New Testament, growing in his ability to understand them and use them in his Christian life. But you can understand a large part of the Gospels now. And you can begin now to make these the center of your reading of the Bible.

For Jesus, more than anyone else in the world, helps us to know our Father. You might read what Jesus himself said about this, as John tells it in John 14:6-10. The better we know Jesus, the better we know our Father who is in heaven. The Bible is our Father's Word, and our Father speaks to us so clearly and plainly through Jesus that Jesus himself is called "the Word." John speaks of that in John 1:1-4.

III

OUR FATHER'S WILL

His Will Is Our Law

WHEN we profess faith in Jesus Christ, we enter the Kingdom of God. In the Kingdom of God, God is King of our hearts and our lives.

When we are in the Kingdom of God we seek to do the will of God. We then *want* to do his will. His will is our law, our highest law, higher than any law. His will is the law we wish to carry in our hearts always, and obey in all that we do.

If we are to keep in training so that we may grow as Christians, we shall seek to do our Father's will. As long as we do his will, we grow as Christians.

What Is Our Father's Will?

But what *is* our Father's will? Every Christian often has to ask that question, and it is an exceedingly important question, for in the Kingdom of God, God needs persons who will *do* his will and not be satisfied when they just talk about it. So we need to know what God's will is.

One way we can answer is to say, "Our Father's will is told us in the Bible." And that is a true answer. We have been trying to know the Bible better, by reading it more thoughtfully, and reading more of it. When we studied about our Father's Word, we saw that the Bible tells us what our Father thinks about us, his children. But the Bible does more than that. It also tells us how we are to think about God, and what God wishes us to be and do.

But when we wish to know what our Father's will is, we cannot use all the different parts of the Bible in exactly the same way. We have to use different ways with different parts of the Bible. The growing Christian needs to learn how to use the various parts of the Bible so that each of us can learn for himself what God's will is.

The Two Parts

As you know, the Bible has two great parts, called the Old Testament and the New Testament. When we are thinking about the will of our Father and are using the Bible to help us know what that will is, there is an easy way to remember the difference between the Old Testament and the New Testament. The Old Testament tells us the law of the Kingdom of God before Jesus came, and the New Testament tells us the law of the Kingdom of God after Jesus came.

There were persons in training in the Kingdom of God long before Jesus came, as well as after he came. But God our Father used one way for them to be in training before Jesus came, and he used a different way after Jesus came. After Jesus came, God used a new way which he had not used before, and the part of the Bible which tells about that new way is called the New Testament.

And when God began to use the new way for the persons in his Kingdom to keep in training as growing members of his Kingdom, some of the old ways he had used for a long time went out of date, as we shall see presently.

When we read the New Testament and learn what it says about the will of God, we know *that* is still the will of God for us now—as for example, the Great Commandments in Matthew 22:37-40. Please find this and read it.

But when we read the Old Testament, we know that not all parts of it are the will of God for us now. Some parts of the Old Testament tell us what God's will for his people was in the old way of training, but these parts are not God's law for Christians now. We shall study more about that presently. Yet there are many parts of the Old Testament that did not go out of date after Jesus came.

If we will compare the two ways of training, we can see the difference, and we can see why some parts of the Old Testament are not God's law for Christians, while other parts of the Old Testament still tell us what God's will for Christians is now.

God's Older Way of Training

In God's older way of training the people in his Kingdom, he followed *the plan of giving laws for everything the people did.* The most important of these laws are in the first five books of the Bible, but especially in the four books of Exodus, Leviticus, Numbers, and Deuteronomy. And the Jewish religious teachers kept adding new laws, besides those in the Bible, until there were many thousands of laws that they said had to be kept. There were 613 laws that were considered especially important, and every person was expected to memorize all 613 so he would be certain to know them and obey them.

There were three kinds of laws in God's older way of training. They are found in the four books named above. Only one of these three kinds of laws is still "in date" as God's will for the Christian members of his Kingdom.

One kind is called the "ceremonial law." The ceremonial law told the people how to conduct their religious ceremonies, such as offering sacrifices and making themselves clean. If you will turn to Leviticus and examine it a few minutes, you will find many laws of that kind. Chapter 1, for example, gives laws that had to be kept in offering sacrifices. Chapter 11 gives examples of laws the people had to observe so they would be considered "clean."

In the older way of training, it was very important for the people to know these ceremonial laws. When a Jewish boy started to school, the book of Leviticus was the very first thing he started to study; and he learned to read by studying Leviticus. But in God's new way of training, for the Christians, these laws are out of date. They are not God's will for us now. However, many of these laws do help Christians to understand the meaning of Christ's death as a sacrifice for us. Hebrews 9:1-14 tells us about this.

A second kind of law in the Old Testament is called "civil law." In the older way of training, God's law included many laws about matters such as our legislatures now deal with. The twenty-fifth chapter of Leviticus is an example, which you might examine. These laws and others of the same class in the Old Testament were kind and just laws, and our legislatures have often passed laws like them. But the civil laws of the Old Testament are out of date now so far as being law is concerned, although they often make us seek for ways of being as kind and as just now as God wished his people to be then.

A third kind of law is called the "moral law." This deals with our relation to God, and our relation to one another. The Ten Commandments are a summary of the moral law. They are in Exodus 20:1-17. Will you read it now? *Moral law is not out of date.* The parts of the Old Testament that tell of the right relation of our hearts to God, and the parts that tell how we should treat our fellow men, are still the will of God for us.

God's Newer Way of Training

In God's newer way of training the people in his Kingdom, he followed *the plan of giving us one law as*

79

his will, instead of many laws, and he expects the members of his Kingdom to take the responsibility of finding the best ways to use that one law in everything we do.

If you will read Matthew 22:34-40, you will see how Jesus came to emphasize the one law with its two parts. He put all the commandments of God into two Great Commandments. The first of these commandments is, "Thou shalt love the Lord thy God with all thy heart, and with all thy soul, and with all thy mind." The second is, "Thou shalt love thy neighbour as thyself." Both these commandments begin, "Thou shalt love . . . ." Love toward God and love toward our "neighbour" are our supreme duty, as Christ taught.

In God's older plan of training, a person grew by learning the many laws of the Old Testament, and keeping them. In God's newer plan, one grows by taking the *one* law of love into his heart, and then finding better ways of using it.

All of the New Testament and much of the Old Testament helps us to do that, by helping us to see what a person does when he uses the law of love in his living.

The best way the New Testament does this is by what Jesus taught and did. He showed us what love means when it is used as much as a person can ever do. For such a person does not just keep a set of laws. Instead, he gives himself up to loving completely, and by loving he grows to be the finest person one can possibly be. Many other parts of the New Testament also help us to see what love in living means. The twelfth chapter of First Corinthians is one example, among many; the thirteenth chapter is another.

Pioneers

Every Christian is, or should be, a pioneer. For we have the one great law which it is our Father's will that we should use every day in everything we do and are. He has not told us every little thing about how to use love in our daily living. He has made us responsible for constantly finding new ways. And each one who finds a better way to express love at home, or at school, or anywhere else, is a Christian pioneer. He is growing by doing the will of the Father.

IV

OUR FATHER'S WORK

A Body That Works Together

SUPPOSE that Saturday morning, when you awoke, some parts of your body had gone on a strike! Imagine that when you tried to rise from bed, one foot had refused to work, because it wanted all the honor of carrying you around on a holiday. You limped over to comb your hair, but one hand refused to co-operate with the other, and as fast as one hand combed, the other rumpled.

In a rather unpresentable state you got to breakfast, but your eyes quarreled, each eye being jealous of the other and trying to do all the looking.

You had a tennis game that morning, and when you got to the court your hands and your feet had a long argument over which wins a tennis game—hands or feet? And for good measure your eyes joined in the dispute, saying, "Where do *we* come in? Just try a tennis game without *us!*"

Foolish as that sounds, it is just what might happen if all the members of the body should refuse to work together for you so that they might carry out your will.

The Body of Christ

In the Bible, the church is compared to a body. It is called the Body of Christ.

The church at Corinth was having trouble because some of the Christians there were jealous of others, and they were quarreling. Paul wrote them a letter, and we still have a copy of it. In the letter he tried to get them to see what would happen in one person's body if the members refused to co-operate.

Then he went on to tell them, When you are members of the church you are members of the Body of Christ. Each member must take his part. If we do that, the church can grow and each one of us can grow. But if we do not take our part, neither we nor the church can grow as we might.

This part of Paul's letter is in I Corinthians 12:12-31. Will you read it?

Then read I Corinthians 13. If your Bible has the word "charity" in this chapter, you may read "love" instead of "charity." For the word "charity" here means "love."

We can see that Paul was teaching the church at Corinth two great things. One is that love is God's highest law, God's will. We studied about that in the last chapter. The other thing is that the church is the Body of Christ, which God wishes to use as a Body through which his law of love can be expressed. If the members of the church refuse to do their part, the church as the Body of Christ cannot live out God's law of love. But if the members of the church do their part, then God has a Body in the world through which he can express his love.

Growing in Our Father's Work

When Jesus was twelve, he said, "I must be about my Father's business." (Luke 2:41-49.) When a young person professes faith in Christ, by his own choice he is taken into the full responsibilities of church membership. Our Father's work then becomes *our* work. Like Jesus, we know the time has come when we must begin to have our responsibilities, each of us, in "our Father's business." Presently we shall think about what some of those responsibilities are.

And if we do our part as members of the church, the church means more to us. For example, a boy was asked to usher one Sunday. After church he remarked, "Mother, I just liked the whole service better today!" And we are likely to feel like that in the church, when we have lived as we should, whether inside the church building or through the week.

One of the ways in which we grow as Christians is by doing our part as members of the church. For it may seem strange, but it is true, that if we do our Father's work, we understand and love our Father himself and his teaching, better. In John 7:16, 17, John tells us that Jesus himself spoke of that. Will you read it?

Keeping Our Pledge

What is our part in our Father's work, as young Christians just taking up our responsibilities for ourselves?

After a person has become fully a member of the church by his own decision, it would be well for him to think often of the pledge he took when he made his profession of faith. Perhaps we can remember the words of the pledge used in our church. If not, we might turn back to the second lesson that you studied in class, and read the one given there. See pages 29 and 30.

In keeping that pledge there are certain things we can do, and certain attitudes we can have. Some of these are mentioned here, but perhaps we shall wish to add others.

Things We Can Do

WE CAN BE REGULAR IN ATTENDANCE. Our church has its services of worship, when the minister preaches, teaches the congregation the meaning of our Father's Word, and leads us in the worship of God. The church has its school, and its young people's meetings. These and the other services of the church are centers for our training and growth as Christians. We need these services, and they need us. If we wish to keep in training as Christians, we need to go regularly where other Christians also are keeping training. Our church needs every member in his place doing his part every Sunday, otherwise our church is not getting the best possible start in its week of work for our Father.

WE CAN GIVE. As soon as we become fully responsible members of the church we should begin to contribute regularly to the work of the church, if we have not already commenced to do so. In that way we begin to carry our part of the cost of the church's work in our home congregation, and we begin to share in our church's work in other parts of the homeland and abroad.

Outside the church, money is often asked for many good causes. It is well to give as we can to other work in our community and beyond, when we are sure it is for a worthy object. But in our giving as Christians we must not forget the church and its work.

Many find it is an excellent habit to set aside a tenth of one's income—allowance, earnings, etc.—to be used for religious purposes. Those who do this usually have something on hand to give whenever they feel they should make a contribution.

WE CAN BE CHRISTIANS IN THE CHURCH. Doing our part as Christians means being Christians in the church as well as at home and elsewhere. A young Christian's conduct in church school class, in other group meetings, and during the service of worship and preaching, is one test of the way he is putting his religion to work. The teachers, the officers of the church, and the minister, cannot do their part fully unless we do ours by courteous and reverent behavior in the church. Every young person can spoil or can help to make the lesson, or the other meetings, or the worship service.

WE CAN BE CHRISTIANS ALL THROUGH THE WEEK. If we have truly begun to be followers of Jesus Christ, the first people who will see a difference in us are the members of our family. If we are no better at home than we were before, those who live there with us may wonder whether becoming a responsible member of the church has really made much difference in us. But if it has, they will know it whether they say so or not.

And being a Christian extends all through the week, at home, at school, with our friends, when we are with strangers, when we see people suffering, when we see people in need. How do you think a Christian will be different from a non-Christian in the presence of needy and suffering people? If we are growing as Christians we shall constantly be seeking ways to carry the law of love with us and put it to work. This part in our Father's work never ends.

WE CAN BRING OTHERS. Very likely each of us has friends who are not members or attendants at any church. We may invite them to come with us to class, to the church service, or to our other meetings. For the church needs to reach out constantly, bringing others to Christ as Lord and Saviour. Often it can reach out through us as young Christians, by such an invitation.

When strangers or newcomers are in the class, or in any of the services, we can help them feel at home. If you have ever gone to a strange church where you knew no one, you remember how much it means to find one person who is friendly and cordial.

Attitudes We Can Have

There are certain attitudes we can cultivate, which will help us in keeping the pledge we made as followers of Christ.

WE CAN BE DEPENDABLE. If we accept a responsibility, we let somebody down unless we carry it out faithfully. We are now in the service of a Leader who never lets anybody down. In this, we can begin to be like him.

WE CAN BE LOYAL. As young Christians we can help to make our pastor, our teacher, our church, our school, stronger by our loyalty. We do not need to go around bragging. But a sincere word spoken in appreciation of what the minister, or the teacher, or the officers of the church do, is something no one of them will forget. Our loyalty is a reward they long to have and are entitled to have, for they are doing their part to help us grow in our Father's work.

WE CAN BE FAIR AND HONEST. We know how much being fair and honest means. We know what fairness means to our group. We know how unfairness spoils a group. It is close to loyalty, isn't it?

Can you think of other attitudes that help us keep our pledge to Christ, other ways we can express our love for Christ?

V

OUR FATHER'S WORSHIP

Every Member Needed

THE CHURCH, the Body of Christ, needs every member doing his part in the work of our Father, as we saw in the last chapter. And in exactly the same way, the Body of Christ needs every member in the worship of our Father.

On Sunday the congregation gathers for worship. We call it by many names, such as the church service, morning and evening worship, the morning service and the evening service, and so on.

The custom of gathering as a congregation, for worship, is as old as the Christian church. For Christians are the Body of Christ and that Body is held together generation after generation by worshipping together in the presence of God.

And just as the work of the body is incomplete unless each member does his part, so the worshipping Body of Christ is not complete unless each member is present and worships as a member of the whole Body.

This is true for the young Christian just as it is for the older Christian. For baptized children and youth are members of the church, as we learned in the class, and the worship is not complete unless they are in the congregation. The service of worship does not belong just to the grown people. It belongs to all who are members of the Body of Christ, whatever their age.

It is true that we often have periods of worship in the Sunday church school by classes or by departments. We worship in other meetings of our group, and at many other times. It is well that we should, and all these times can be of great value to us. We wish to take our part as well and as worthily as we can. But none of these takes the place of the worship of the entire congregation, when the whole Body as one Body presents itself before God. The church at worship needs each member present.

But each member also needs the worship if he is to continue growing as a Christian. And now we are to consider how it is that worship helps the Christian to grow.

Relighting the Fire

On a Southern plantation, one Sunday morning, the owner was riding down the road when he met an old Negro. They stopped to talk. The conversation was long, and as they talked, a church bell began to ring. The old Negro grew restless, and at last he said, "I've got to go now. I've got to go down the road there, where that bell's ringin', and light my candle at God's fire."

This old man had found what worship can mean in our living, and he had put it in that simple way. During the week we are busy with many things. Our bodies and our spirits grow weary. Presently we begin to forget things we ought to remember, and not to see things that we ought to see, such as the beauty of the earth, or the needs of people near us who are tired or discouraged. Even when the work we are doing is our Father's work, we need to rest and worship again, so that we may again have the "fire" in us kindled by coming into God's presence as a part of the Body which is being refreshed.

The Service

The service of worship is not the same in all churches. Often it is helpful to know what is done in other churches. But first of all we should recall what is done in the service in *our* church. Perhaps you could write the order of service as the minister uses it. Or if your church publishes a bulletin, you might examine the one to be used this Sunday.

We should try to understand the purpose of each part in the service. We might ask two questions concerning each part in the service. "Why is this done?" And, "What should the members of the congregation do during this part of the service?"

Then we might see that at least four kinds of things are usually done in our services of worship. They are the prayers, the preaching, the giving, and the singing. Suppose we take these in turn, and ask, "How may this help young Christians to grow?"

The Prayers

In the next chapter we are to think of our personal friendship with God, in our prayer life as growing Christians. But just now we are thinking of the prayers offered by the minister. How may these help the young Christian to grow?

For one thing, the minister's prayers help us as young Christians because he often mentions us in his prayer. Sometimes we feel that God is answering the minister's prayer for us, right then and there. At other times we look back and see that God has already been answering some of those prayers, for a long time. And always it makes us grateful that the pastor of the church prays to God in our behalf. In Philippians 1:3-11 you can read one minister's prayer for his people, knowing that often our minister offers just such prayer for us, remembering us by name, and asking God to supply our needs.

The minister's prayer may help us to grow as young Christians, because when he is offering prayer, often we learn from him how *we* might pray. We need not try to use just the same words he does, for our prayer may be in our own words. But the minister in his prayer helps us to be reverent toward God when we pray, and he helps us to see some of the things that it is fitting we should speak about in our prayer.

If the minister's prayer is to help us in these ways, we need to listen carefully, and pray with him in our hearts for the same things, while he prays.

The Preaching

When the minister preaches, he is our teacher. He reads a "lesson" from the Bible. Then he takes a text, explains it, and shows us what it means for our living. Or perhaps he takes some difficulty which many of us are facing, and shows us how we can meet that difficulty as Christians and overcome it. Or perhaps he shows us some better way of living which we had never thought about, but which we wish to follow as soon as we see it.

No two ministers preach alike, for there are as many ways of preaching as there are ministers. But the minister has given years of study to our Father's Word, and each time he preaches he shows us how to understand that Word better, or how to live in a more Christian way.

If the preaching is to help us grow, we need to listen carefully every moment, so that we shall not miss anything that we might take with us and put to work in our lives. As the minister begins to preach, one might say within himself, "I expect God to say something to *me* today through this sermon. I shall keep myself alert, so I shall hear it. And I ask God to help me do whatever he wishes."

As you listen to the sermon next time, think of these things. Try to think how the things the minister says apply to you. Try to think as the minister preaches, "What is God saying to me through my minister and this sermon today?"

The Giving

Giving is one of the ways in which we worship.

Sometimes, as young Christians, we are tempted to think, "What I can give is so small that it is not important." But Jesus taught us that God does not think of giving in that way. In Mark 12:41-44 there is a story about Jesus which shows that he was greatly interested in seeing how people put their money into the offering. Will you read it? Through that story we are shown that God measures the importance of our gift, not by its size in dollars and cents, but by discovering how much it means to the one who is giving.

So the Christian needs to grow in his giving, as he does in other ways. Certainly the size of the gifts should increase as we are able to give more. But it is more important that we should learn to give as a way of expressing our love. As we learn to do that, the giving Christian becomes a growing Christian.

The Singing

The hymns are among the richest treasures of the Christian church. They take many of the very thoughts that are in the Bible and in our beliefs, and express them, and we can sing them with a new understanding.

The hymns are the voice of Christian men and women of every age. Many of these persons knew trouble and suffering, but they also knew God, and they triumphed over difficulties until they could sing because of the joy they had. The hymn "O Love That Wilt Not Let Me Go" is one of that kind. The author, Dr. Matheson, a blind minister, was sitting in the manse one evening alone. Something had happened which made him feel deeply discouraged. But suddenly an idea came, which made him rise above the thought of his blindness. In five minutes he wrote a hymn which millions have sung since. Read the stanzas of this hymn.

The hymns can help us to grow in our understanding and love of God, and in our desire to live as a Christian should. But if they are to serve us in that way, there are certain things we need to do, ourselves.

We should sing with the congregation, if we can sing. If we cannot sing, then we can read the words as the hymn is being sung.

We should think about the hymn that is being sung, so that we can sing it "from the heart." Some people say that if we *think* about what we are singing, that is one sign we are growing past childhood in our religion.

And we should grow familiar with the greater, better hymns, and pay less attention to those that are inferior.

VI

OUR FATHER'S FRIENDSHIP

Communing with God

Do you remember the story of Jack Redmon, who found an old diary written by his father? And do you remember how Jack used to say, "Oh, I wish I could have known him myself"?

Many times when we think of our Father in heaven whom we cannot see, there comes a longing like that. We wish we could know him as a child knows his father, or as a person knows his closest friend. We can read about him in the Bible, and we can learn about him from the worship and teaching of the church. Yet we want to know him, ourselves.

And it *is* possible to know him, in the friendship with God which we call prayer. We never see him with our eyes, but we may think about him and commune with him in our hearts.

To commune with God means to share our thoughts with God. Sometimes we also speak of this as fellowship with God. And it is a friendship which can grow, if we let it, until it is the richest friendship which a Christian can ever have. This is one of the best of all ways to stay in training as a Christian.

The Lord's Prayer

The Lord's Prayer is the noblest of all prayers, and of course every Christian should know it. In praying the Lord's Prayer we should think of what we are saying. When we are alone, it is helpful to pray this prayer aloud, slowly, thinking of each phrase. Will you read it in Matthew 6:9-13? Then let us take each petition separately, and think of the meaning of what is said.

Our Father which art in heaven.

> He is in heaven. He is everywhere. He is with us, and in us. And yet he is far beyond us. From our hearts, and homes, and churches, out to the limits of the last star, he is there.

Hallowed be thy name.

> Hallowed means "be made holy," or "be treated as holy." Our Father is holy, and we pray that we and all persons may think of him, speak about him, and act toward him, with reverence.

Thy kingdom come.

> We pray that God may be the King and Father of every heart, that we and all people everywhere may make him the one and only Ruler of our lives.

Thy will be done in earth, as it is in heaven.

> His will is our highest law. We pray that we and all people everywhere may obey that will in earth as the souls of the departed do in heaven and as we shall do there. But we ask that we may be helped to obey it today, here and now.

Give us this day our daily bread.

The food we eat, the water we drink, the clothes we wear, warmth for our bodies, sunshine and air, all the great and simple gifts of "nature," are gifts of God to his children. We and others toil for many of these, but that willingness to labor, and the earth itself that brings forth her increase, are God's gifts. May a portion suited to our need be given us today.

And forgive us our debts, as we forgive our debtors.

Forgive us for the sins we have committed. We pledge thee that today we forgive those who have sinned against us. We come now with all grudges wiped out from our hearts. And as we have forgiven others, we ask to be forgiven, ourselves.

And lead us not into temptation, but deliver us from evil.

Let us not be put in any temptation that is too great for us to bear. When we are tempted to do any wrong, make our minds quick to see how we can escape from that temptation, and make our wills strong so that we shall leave that temptation while we can.

For thine is the kingdom, and the power, and the glory, for ever. Amen.

(This petition is not in all the old copies of the Gospel of Matthew, hence in the Bible that you use it may be in the margin only.)

The Kingdom, the rule, of all the universe and all people belongs to thee and only to thee, our Father. Thou hast the power to bring thy will to pass. Thine is the only true glory in heaven or on earth.

"Amen" means "may it be so."

Sharing Our Thoughts with God

If we look back upon what we have just been thinking and saying, we can see that prayer may begin with talking to God, but if we are really thinking about what we are saying when we pray, we find we are thinking faster than we can speak. That *thinking* is prayer, too, just as truly as if we put it all into words.

And as we grow in knowing how to pray, we discover that we wish to *think* much of our private prayer, and that we do not have to stop always to say it in words. Often, of course, we do want to take time to say it. But we do not have to *say* it, for it to be prayer. We can *think* our prayer.

As we learn to think our prayer, we discover that we do not have to use just one time in the day to pray. We can pray in our hearts as often as it comes into our minds to do so. Most Christians who grow in discovering what prayer can be, wish to have a certain time in the day when they keep the habit of praying. But our prayer can take place all through the day, too, at any time.

What Thoughts May We Share?

Any thoughts we have are thoughts we may share with the Father. Thoughts that we cannot share with him are not good to think about or to keep for ourselves. And often, thinking of him will drive away thoughts that have no rightful place in our hearts.

But there are certain kinds of thinking which it is especially suitable that we should share with the Father in heaven, in our prayer. We may say them completely in words if we wish, or we may think them more rapidly as prayer-thoughts. A young Christian does well to try both ways.

THINKING OF GOD. A good way to begin our prayer is by thinking of all the things we like, the things that make us happy, the things that give us fun and joy. For each one we give thanks to God. This is the prayer of gratitude, or of thanks. An example of prayer of this kind in the Bible may be read in Psalm 46, or in Psalm 103.

And as we give thanks, often our feeling of love for God our Father grows, until we wish to say, "I love thee, Father, for these good things that have been given to me." Sometimes older Christians call this "adoration," especially when they think of the kind of God our Father is— powerful, fair, and good. An example of this sort of prayer is in Psalm 18:1, 2; and in Psalm 93. These should be read.

THINKING ABOUT OURSELVES. In our prayer it is right to think about ourselves, if we can do this in a way that is not selfish, but that helps us to be better, growing Christians.

Each day we need to be cleansed of our sins. We should make our prayer of confession, briefly telling God the things we have said, or done, or thought, that were sinful; and asking God for the sake of Christ to forgive all our sins. Then we should accept God's forgiveness, not continuing to think about our sin, but believing and knowing that God has forgiven. An instance of a prayer of this kind is the publican's prayer, as given in Luke 18:9-14. You may read that prayer.

And we may ask God for whatever we really need. We may talk to him about our needs. This part of our prayer is called "petition," or asking for changes in ourselves, as when we ask God to help us be more thoughtful. Jesus encouraged prayer of this kind, as told in Matthew 7:7-11; and he taught us to pray in his name, as we are told in John 16:23, 24. These may be read also.

God will answer this prayer. Yet we must understand that he may not always answer us in just the way we asked him to do. If God did everything exactly as we asked him to do, God would be doing *our* will. We cannot expect him to do that, but we can ask, "*Thy* will be done."

Sam Horton was a boy who saw this difference. Friday night before a baseball game on Saturday, he prayed, "Father in heaven, don't let it rain tomorrow, please, for Jesus' sake. Amen." His mother, hearing the prayer, said, "Sam, some of the farmers need rain badly, and I think they are praying for rain so their crops will be saved. I wonder what God will do about all these different prayers?"

Sam thought hard for a minute. Then he said, "Mother, I think I'll tell God just to use his own judgment about it." That is nearly the same thing that we mean when we say in our prayer, "Thy will be done."

THINKING ABOUT OTHERS. In our prayer we should go beyond ourselves and our own needs, to think of others. This is the prayer of "intercession," or "asking God for others."

We may think of one person at a time, until we have included as many as we wish. As we think of any person, we may ask, "What does he need most?" And we may ask God to supply that need in any way he sees fit; in this also remembering that God is wiser than we, and asking that *his* will shall be done.

Often, during such praying, we realize there is something we might do to help our Father meet the needs of our friends. Very often we can help God answer our prayers.

Listening

Prayer, as we have seen, is sharing our thoughts with God. But it can be much more even than that. We can be sure that many, many times God also wishes to share *his* thoughts with *us*. He wants us to know his thoughts of us and his will for us.

So it is well, often, to let prayer be a time of listening. This is like being in a conversation with a friend—we have to give the friend a chance to speak! Sometimes we will cease talking to God in prayer, we try even to cease thinking about God, and we let our minds be just as quiet as we can.

And often God will speak to us when our hearts are quiet and still in prayer. Of course we do not actually hear his voice. But he may speak to us through the thoughts that come to us when we have ceased talking to him and our hearts are waiting.

Perhaps we have been praying for some friend of ours. Then in the listening moment the thought comes, "I could *do* so and so for my friend." Perhaps that is God's voice speaking.

In our listening moments, we may think of something we have neglected to do, or of some person who is lonely and needs friendship. That may be God's voice speaking.

In our prayer perhaps we have been asking God to help us know what is right to do about something that puzzles us. In the listening moments perhaps we remember our pledge of loyalty to our Leader, and we remember the kind of person we meant to be when we took those pledges. Then, often, we suddenly see what we ought to do about that thing that puzzled us so. That may be God's voice speaking.

A Growing Friendship

These are only *suggestions* for our prayer. We do not have to pray in any one manner. We should feel as free in our communion with our Father as we do in any companionship with other very dear friends.

For prayer is a friendship with God, our King and our Father. And as with every true friendship, this one will grow if we let it and if we do our part.

VII
OUR FATHER'S KINGDOM

"I Wonder!"

As WE PASS from childhood to youth, we begin to think more about the things that are happening in our state, in our nation, and in the great world still further away.

We have our own part to take at home, in the church, at school, and in the community. But out beyond all that are events that set older people talking, events that we read about in newspapers, hear about on the radio, and hear people discussing.

For our world is now in one of those periods of upheaval such as we study about in our history, when barbarian nations overran the countries they wanted, and old civilizations passed away. One time of that kind came when the Christian church was young and the Roman Empire was breaking up. Another came with the French Revolution.

In the lifetime of those who now are young, there have been especially great changes. Nations that once were strong have passed out of existence, and weak ones have grown powerful. New forms of government are spreading. Different ways of thinking are competing for the mastery of the entire world. Probably the history books of the future will speak of these years as one of the greatest revolutions in all history.

Hearing of the things taking place and thinking about them, many young persons are saying, "I wonder what part *I* should have in these events as I grow old enough to do anything about it?"

And sometimes, especially when older people are discouraged and fearful, we think, "I wonder how it is all coming out?"

Young Christians *should* ask questions of that kind. Finding the answers wisely, and living wisely by the answers we find, helps to bring growth within us as Christians, and helps us to do our part in our world as Christians should.

Perhaps these things about which we shall think today will help us in finding some of our answers.

The Two Kingdoms

We have already studied about the Kingdom of God. We are in the Kingdom of God when we profess faith in Christ, and sincerely desire and try to let God's will, the law of love, be the law of life for us. We then are under the rule, or Kingship, of God.

But in the Bible we are taught that there are two Kingdoms. One is the Kingdom of God. The other is a kingdom called by different names, such as "the power of darkness." It is a Kingdom of Evil. Its laws are laws of deceit, hatred, cruelty, and force.

At times the Kingdom of Evil gains tremendous power, overrunning the earth, killing, maiming, destroying, causing grievous suffering even to the followers of Christ.

But the Kingdom of Evil cannot finally win, for God is on the side of the Kingdom of Love. We do not know how every battle in the conflict is coming out, but we do know that the long conflict itself will go in favor of the Kingdom of God. For love is stronger than hatred, and Christ is more powerful than any person or any force or any nation that opposes him. The Kingdom of God is the only Kingdom that can finally win and keep on winning.

We must understand that the struggle between the Kingdom of God and the Kingdom of Evil is not the same as the struggle between any two nations. No one nation is completely in the Kingdom of God, and no one nation is completely in the Kingdom of Evil.

We can understand this better if we remember how it is in our own life. If we are Christians, sincerely making God the Ruler of our life, we are in the Kingdom of God; yet always evil has some power within us, for no one of us can keep the law of God perfectly. It is the same with nations.

A Partnership

The Kingdom of God is, in one way, a partnership between God and us. We must do our part to put the law of love into daily living; for, as we learned, the church is the Body of Christ, a Body through which God's will can be expressed among men.

But God gives the victory where we could never win it by ourselves. For the Bible teaches us that God will consummate his Kingdom. That means he will bring it through to completeness. We do not know when his Kingdom will be complete and perfect. We only know that it *will* be. So in the Lord's Prayer we pray, "Thy kingdom come."

In a partnership such as this, we know that God counts on us, as followers of Christ, to express the law of love in daily living.

What Can I Do About It?

Let's go back and think again now of the question many people ask when the world is in upheaval—"What can I do about it?"

Of course there are many things about which we can do nothing at all, except pray. As Christians, we *can* remember to do that, daily. And if we keep up the practice of prayer regarding world events, this takes away much of the feeling of helplessness, for we remember each day that we are on God's side, that we are trying to do his will, and that our Father is Maker and Ruler of heaven and earth. Often, in this prayer, we do not know what to ask, for as Paul wrote, "We know not what we should pray for as we ought." But we can always ask, "Father, cause thy Kingdom to come, cause the Kingdom of Evil to be defeated, and cause me to be ready today to do anything that comes my way to do as a citizen of the Kingdom of God."

What kind of things will come our way? *Every moment we are with another person is a moment when we can live in keeping with the law of the Kingdom of God, which is the law of love.* Perhaps it will help you to see this if you read Matthew 25:31-46.

In this passage, Jesus is speaking of what is called the Judgment Day. People whose earthly lives have been lived and ended, are in the presence of the King. He is to decide whether they are to go into the eternal Kingdom of God or into the eternal Kingdom of Darkness. Their relationship to Christ, as shown in the way they have lived, determines which Kingdom they shall enter eternally.

Jesus is teaching us here that our profession of love for him and our faith in him must be followed by living in obedience to the law of the Kingdom, the law of love, if we are to enter the eternal Kingdom of God.

But notice the kind of things he chose in deciding whether they had used the law of the Kingdom of God in living. These are examples of the kindly, thoughtful acts we can do every moment we are with other persons. When we do these, we are serving Christ, as he taught us in this passage.

Notice, too, that it requires imagination to see how the other person feels, to see what his needs are, and to know how to meet that need. Jesus gave us a remarkable saying, called the Golden Rule, to show us that we need to use imagination in our treatment of other people. He said, "All things therefore whatsoever ye would that men should do unto you, even so do ye also unto them." (Matthew 7:12, A. S. V.)

And in this parable of the Judgment we can see something of what Jesus meant by the Golden Rule. For instance, Jesus said, "I was a stranger, and ye took me in." A "stranger" is not just a newcomer, but any person who is lonely, without friends and kindness. They are anywhere, perhaps in your own home. Have you ever felt like a stranger? Then you know how others feel.

Who are people like the prisoners, the sick, the hungry, the naked, of whom Jesus spoke? We must use our imagination, but when we do we shall find them.

Whenever we carry the law of the Kingdom, the law of love, into daily living, we have "done something about it" in a world trying to decide whether to live by the law of the Kingdom of God or that of the Kingdom of Evil.

You can help prove to our world that the law of the Kingdom of God works, and is better to live by than the law of the Kingdom of Evil.

Part Three

FOR THE PASTOR

As a minister, you have had long training in the subjects with which these lessons deal, and it seems superfluous to offer any helps for teaching. But many do desire suggestions for teaching this particular kind of course. For that reason, and also because the plan of "supervised study" has been followed in preparing the material, Part Three is provided for those who may wish to use it. Experience has shown that this approach enlists the boys and girls in the study of the course, so that they are not merely listeners. It is taken for granted, and is strongly urged, that any minister using these suggestions will also use full liberty in adapting them.

Church Membership

The boys and girls in your class may stand in either of two possible relationships to the church.

First, there are the persons who have been baptized in infancy, but have not yet made their own profession of faith. In the language of the church, these are called "children of the covenant." According to the doctrines of the Presbyterian Church, these children are already members of the church. Before they can be admitted to the full responsibilities and privileges of the church, they must make their own profession of faith. But we cannot invite them to "join the church," for they are members already. In the terms which the church uses, they may be invited to profess faith in Christ and be admitted to the Lord's Supper. If one does that, he becomes a communicant member, that is, one entitled to partake of the Communion.

SECOND, there are persons who have not been baptized in infancy, and who have not yet made profession of faith in Christ. It is fitting not only to invite them to profess faith, but also to "join the church."

Both the first and the second of these groups still have to make profession of faith before being admitted to full membership in the church. The common element in our aim for both groups is the profession of faith in Christ. But the present relationship to the church differs as between the first group and the second.

Whatever the relation of the boys and girls to the church when they enter the class, it is your privilege to be an "Ambassador of Christ" in a peculiarly intimate way during this course. This is an evangelistic opportunity of a unique kind.

Problems in Adaptation

Your work will need to be constantly adapted in keeping with two principles. We shall wish to discover and build upon what has already been accomplished in the lives of these boys and girls, in family and in church, so that they may be led on from the point they have already reached in their own relation to Christ and his church. And we must be ready, always, to take time for the most elementary explanations. You may find misunderstanding concerning things where you would least expect it.

Materials

The following materials will be needed:

A copy of the booklet for each pupil.

A Bible for each pupil.

A copy of the Westminster Standards, containing the Confession of Faith, the Larger Catechism, the Shorter Catechism, and the Book of Church Order.

A copy of *A Manual of Faith and Life,* by Hugh T. Kerr.

Memory Work

There are five items of suggested memory work:

The Apostles' Creed

The Ten Commandments, Exodus 20:1-17

The Great Commandments, Matthew 22:37-40

The Golden Rule, Matthew 7:12

The Lord's Prayer, Matthew 6:9-13

For many centuries the Apostles' Creed, the Ten Commandments, and the Lord's Prayer have been associated with the occasion of public confession of faith in Christ and reception into the church.

The Westminster Shorter Catechism is a summary of "the Presbyterian Creed." In some churches it will be possible to have this catechism memorized as "Honors Memory Work." To learn this great document of Protestant theology thoroughly and intelligently puts one in possession of a great treasure. The time when a child of the covenant is preparing for admission to the Lord's Supper is ordinarily the most suitable of all times for its memorization, especially if the person is of Intermediate or Senior age.

But this catechism should be learned intelligently if at all. To memorize it merely for the sake of saying it has been memorized, or merely to get a reward, is of limited value. It should be learned for its own sake, as a great masterpiece is learned. It should be explained carefully. For such reasons, we do not advise trying to crowd the Shorter Catechism memory work into an already brief lesson period. Let it be done in added periods, with those boys and girls who will come willingly, and by teachers who willingly give the added time, for the sake of learning and teaching one of the greatest documents ever written to express "what man is to believe concerning God, and what duty God requires of man."

I

FOLLOWERS OF CHRIST

THE AIM of this first lesson is: To refresh the memory of the boys and girls by a recall of the entire life story of Jesus; to help them see some of the reasons they can more readily understand, which led him to give up his life; to help them see what it meant to follow him in the days when he was on earth and immediately afterward; and to lead them to consider our need of him and his need of followers today.

Some, and perhaps all, of your pupils have heard of Jesus from their earliest days. But much of what they have learned has been in fragments. Few will have a sense of the life of Christ as a connected whole. There may be some in your group to whom any acquaintance with Christ at all is a relatively new experience. For such reasons the larger part of the first session is given over to relating the story of Jesus' life as a whole.

It seems likely that we can help boys and girls to enter more sympathetically into the meaning of Jesus' life and death if we show them how genuine, how real, the problems in Jesus' own mind were as he sought to carry out his mission. When we ask them to follow Jesus Christ, we want them to see that he was utterly loyal himself, loyal even to the end, even though it cost life itself. We want them at least to begin to glimpse the fact that for Jesus, death was not defeat, but triumph. If they can get hold of that idea and make it their own, all later meanings which they see in his life, and in following him, should be richer for it. It is not necessary to try to put all our theology into this first lesson. Present Jesus winsomely and they will want a theology!

Suggestions for Class Procedure

APPROACH TO THE LESSON. You might begin by asking, "Can you remember when you heard about Jesus for the very first time?" Sum up the replies. The purpose here is to bring out the fact, as far as it is a fact, that the pupils have known of Jesus Christ from the beginning of their lives, and have continued to learn of him as they grew. And if the situation in your class is otherwise, this gives you opportunity to know it.

THE STORY OF JESUS. Then you might say to the group something like this:

You have known about Jesus for a long time, and you have learned of him each year as you grew. But if someone were to ask you to tell the story of the life of Jesus from the time he was born until he left the earth, you might find that you did not know the story of his life very clearly. In our study we are going to think about "Becoming a Christian." Today we are going to begin by thinking about "Followers of Christ." And it would be a good thing if we could hear the story of his whole life at one time, before we begin to think about the people who followed him when he was here, and before we think about the way people today can follow him now. So we are going to have a story of the whole life of Jesus. And as you hear the story think about this: The followers of Jesus had to do more than just know about him. Many people knew about him without being his followers. His followers made up their minds to trust him, to believe that what he said was true, and to obey him when he told them to act.

After the story is read, you will need to be sensitive to the response of the class. It may be that the mood of worship will result. If so, capture the mood and give opportunity for spontaneous but very brief expression of it.

Whether you have worship at this point or not, it may be the pupils will wish to discuss the story. If so, welcome the comments. This will allow you to know the impressions made, and to clear up any possible misunderstanding of words or of events.

FOLLOWERS OF JESUS. Ask one of the pupils to read the first paragraph of this section. If you wish, you may have the pupils look up two passages which bring out the fact that Jesus called disciples to go with him and learn from him—Matthew 4:18-23 and Mark 3:13-15.

ALTERNATIVE PROCEDURES. You may choose between two possible procedures for developing the remainder of this lesson. The first will conserve time; the second has the advantage of using more the directed-study method, if time permits.

1. Have the next seven paragraphs read, perhaps having each one read by a different person. Then, if you wish, you may ask the pupils to find certain passages. As each one is read, ask the pupils to decide which of Jesus' requirements this illustrates. Use the passages in chance order, so the pupils cannot answer by merely following the quarterly. Some suitable passages are these: Luke 8:25, trust. Matthew 10:24, 25, loyalty. Matthew 11:29; Mark 4:10, 11; Luke 10:22, learning. Matthew 10:5-7, action. Matthew 9:9, both obedience and action. Matthew 10:37, love; you may need to explain that Jesus wished his disciples to love him so greatly that they would be willing to leave all others and follow him.

2. Ask the pupils to close books after reading and discussing the first paragraph of this section. You might then say, "Jesus expected much of his disciples. Let us see how many things we can think of. What are some of the things Jesus expected his followers to do?" Perhaps the pupils will contribute statements such as "obey him," "be loyal to him," and so on. List whatever is said. Then you might say, "Perhaps we can find out, in the Bible, what Jesus expected of his followers." Ask for the reading of the passages listed in the preceding paragraph. After each has been read, ask, "What does this show that Jesus expected?" When you have finished, your list might read "trust, loyalty, learning, action, obedience, love."

Then have the last three paragraphs of the section read. Two points stand out here: The followers of Jesus became "the church"; and after he was gone from the earth, his followers were expected to meet the same requirements of trust, and so on. Be sure the pupils get the sense of continuity here.

TODAY. Have the two paragraphs of the last section read. This material is in very general terms. Later lessons will make it more specific. But if time allows, ask two questions for discussion: "Why do people need to become followers of Jesus today?" And, "What are some of the ways in which followers of Jesus are needed in our community today?" You can direct the discussion so as to bring out some of the aspects of your own community where the need for Christian ways of living is most apparent.

II
PROFESSION OF FAITH

THE AIM of this lesson is to help the boys and girls to distinguish different relationships one may have to the church; to understand the meaning of making profession of faith in Christ; and to know what is done when one makes his profession of faith.

While it is important to try to make clear to the group that some of them are (baptized) members of the church already, the emphasis of the study as a whole should be on making profession of faith, so that they may understand what it means, and how it is done.

Some may tell you, during this period, that they are ready to make their own profession. A later lesson will definitely carry the aim of securing decisions. Today's lesson is aimed at getting more familiar with the step itself. Other lessons of this course need to be considered by your group before you ask whether they are ready.

In today's lesson the principal emphasis is placed on the meaning of profession of faith in Christ. Faith has two great kinds of meanings in the New Testament. One is *faith in a Person*. The earliest confessions of faith in Christ, as given in the New Testament, were primarily of this nature. Here we are attempting to center the thinking of the boys and girls on this meaning of faith in Christ.

In its second meaning, faith embraces what we believe *about* Christ. The next lesson will deal with that meaning.

APPROACH TO THE LESSON. You might ask, "How many of you have seen a baby baptized?" "What did the minister do?"

"How many of you were baptized when you were babies?" You will probably have this information already. But if some do not know whether they were baptized in infancy, ask them to find out before next Sunday.

"Have any of you felt that you wanted to be followers of Jesus?" Explain that the time when people go before the Session and are received into full membership in the church is called "making profession of faith." That is the way we publicly become followers of Jesus.

JOINING THE CHURCH. Ask for the reading of the first three paragraphs. Be sure the class "gets" the conception that baptized children are members of the church, but are not yet fully members.

Ask for the fourth paragraph to be read. Allow questions, if there are any.

PROFESSION OF FAITH. Assign the paragraphs to various persons to read. Invite discussion where the meaning is not clear. Then you might ask the pupils to answer in their own words: "What does 'profession' mean?" "What did Jesus expect of his followers?" This is a memory question from the last lesson. Make it clear that when boys and girls trust Jesus as Saviour and Friend, are loyal to him, and so on, that is having faith in Jesus now, just as it was then.

You cannot foresee exactly the turn the discussion will now take. It is well to be ready for several possibilities. You will wish to be sure that two things are accomplished. First, you will want to be certain the class understands that making profession of faith is the one thing all persons are asked to do, and will want to do, in order to become followers of Jesus publicly. And second, you will wish to be sure your pupils connect the idea of "faith" with such attitudes of confidence, trust, loyalty, willingness to obey, and so on, as they may already have toward Christ.

OUR LORD. Assign the paragraph to be read, encouraging discussion. For example, you might ask, "How did Jesus want to be King?" "What does a leader do that makes him a leader?"

OUR SAVIOUR. This section may be read, pausing for such questions as the pupils may raise. Pupils may find the passages cited, and answer the questions asked. This gives you the opportunity to supplement the material in whatever way you feel is needed by your particular group. But as the discussion ends, see that the two relations stand out: Jesus Christ as our Lord, and Jesus Christ as our Saviour.

BORN AGAIN. When this section is read, you may need to supplement it so that the two ideas stand out, but in your own words: (1) the necessity of regeneration, and

(2) the signs of regeneration. Since regeneration is wholly God's act, it probably is better in dealing with persons of younger ages to concentrate attention on the fact that certain signs allow us to believe that regeneration has taken place. The work of the Spirit will also be studied in connection with baptism.

MAKING A PROFESSION. Have this section read. Give any necessary encouragement to pupils who draw back from the thought of going to talk the matter over with their parents, or privately with the minister.

THE EXAMINATION. Have the first two paragraphs read. It would help your pupils if you could tell them about the times when the Session of your church prefers that profession of faith should be made, and inform them exactly about arrangements of this kind in your congregation.

Then have the rest of this section read. The purpose is to acquaint the pupils with typical questions asked in the examination. Be sure they understand that *your* questions are the ones they are to answer.

PUBLIC RECEPTION. Perhaps the customs in your church, in this matter, are thoroughly familiar to your class; if not, they can quickly be made clear by you.

Looking Ahead

As for materials, aside from the Bible and manuals, you will need *The Confession of Faith* and *A Manual of Faith and Life*.

The Apostles' Creed will be taken up in the next lesson. If you can have copies ready to distribute today, you might ask the pupils to read it each day this week, and see if they can repeat it at the next meeting. Tell them to be ready to ask questions about the things in the Creed they do not understand, or things in it they wish to discuss.

III
THE CREED

THE AIM of this lesson is to lead the boys and girls to a deeper appreciation of the importance of Christian beliefs, and of the relation of these beliefs to everyday life; to help them know how and where their church's beliefs are expressed; and to arouse their desire to know these beliefs of the church better.

When a boy or girl is considering the dedication of himself to Christ, he is getting his spiritual bearings, seeing where the things are that count most. We certainly wish our boys and girls to be led into Christian action in living, but we also wish them to have that activity rooted down in beliefs, so they can take their bearings by the great mountain peaks of Christian conviction.

The young are already immersed in a world which desperately needs majestic beliefs, great enough to live by and die by. They are on the threshold of fully responsible participation in that world. If they are to be truly Christian *pioneers* in it, they must be rooted and grounded in great convictions, beliefs that are strong enough to stand in any day into which they may ever have to go.

THE IMPORTANCE OF BELIEFS. Have the paragraphs read, one by one. After each reading allow time for discussion. In connection with the third and fourth paragraphs, draw from the pupils illustrations from their own experience, helping them thus to see that their beliefs give direction to their living. For example, "What questions have you had to decide recently about something that you were not sure whether you should do or not? Why did you decide as you did?"

Be sure the class senses how urgent this problem of final loyalty is, in a large part of the world; and be sure they see that their beliefs guide their daily living.

"I BELIEVE." Ask that the material be read by paragraphs. Help the pupils to see that the early followers of Jesus were enthusiastic about him because they knew him well and believed in him deeply.

If your class wishes to see some of the very earliest confessions of faith, have them look up the following passages: Philippians 2:11; I Corinthians 12:3; Romans 10:9. In I Corinthians 15:3, 4, they can see that Paul refers to the teaching which he gave converts; and they can see how similar it is to the language of the creeds.

If the class asks why the convert in the example cited was baptized three times, tell them this was the custom for a while, and still is in some churches. It probably was meant to give emphasis to each of the three persons of the Trinity.

THE APOSTLES' CREED. In this section the pupils should have the feeling of discovering that the familiar Apostles' Creed came out of experiences very like their own as they prepare to confess Christ before men. For, as they should observe, the Apostles' Creed contains statements just like the ones that the pupils were reading in the section entitled "I Believe." This creed was a confession of faith, made at the time when a convert was baptized.

The Creed in its simplest forms probably was passed on from person to person, by word of mouth, long before it was written down. Indeed, for a time it was kept secret from the world, and became a sort of password; people who knew the Creed could prove by repeating it that they were Christians.

The first two paragraphs may be read by individuals. Then ask the entire class to read the Creed in unison, slowly. If time permits, compare it phrase by phrase with the convert's confession in the previous section. Ask that it be read slowly again. Then ask the class to close books and repeat the Creed in unison. After that, ask one or two to repeat it individually. Then go through the Creed to see where further explanation of meaning is necessary. By this time your class should be tingling with questions. If so, welcome that fact. Hushing difficult questions, or sidetracking them, is not permitted! Getting the class hungry for more information is "half the battle" in this lesson.

Assign the Apostles' Creed as memory work, to be called for at the next meeting. Suggest that it be said at least once daily, very slowly, thinking of each phrase before going to the next.

THE PRESBYTERIAN CREED. If appropriate, make the transition by saying that Christians have always been asking such questions as we have been asking today. Request the reading of the section. Then you might add something like this:

In England about three hundred years ago a great many people were asking questions about the church, about God, Christ, the Holy Spirit, and matters of that kind. It was almost like our election times, except that they were talking about the way the church should be governed, and about the creeds. They wanted a form of church government that could be used in all of England, Scotland, and Ireland. So about a hundred and fifty men were appointed to prepare a form of church government, forms for worship, and a creed. They were to submit their work to Parliament for approval. Many of these men were learned scholars. They met in London, and kept meeting for about five years and a half. They held more than a thousand meetings, carefully discussing every point. It was these men who prepared the Presbyterian Creed which you have just been reading about.

Then, if possible, use an actual copy of *The Confession of Faith* itself. Open it to show the location of the four parts mentioned. After the book has been examined by the class, you might wish to say something of this kind:

This book is the Constitution of the Presbyterian Church. The Presbyterian Church, when it ordains ministers, or elders, or deacons, asks them if they believe this creed is true. But that question is not asked when people make profession of faith. For the chief thing the Presbyterian Church wishes to know when one comes to make profession of faith is, "Do you believe in Jesus Christ as your Lord and Saviour?" But that is not all our church *hopes* we will do. It is not all the church *asks* us to do. Let's read the last part of the lesson, and see what the church *invites* us to do when we make profession of faith, and to keep on doing afterward.

GROWING IN OUR BELIEFS. The last section may now be read. Here is your oportunity to help your pupils translate today's work into something they can begin at once to do.

You can suggest two ways for the pupils to begin learning more of the great beliefs of the church, hoping that each pupil will choose at least one.

The first is the study of the Shorter Catechism. And second, you might suggest that the pupils carefully read *A Manual of Faith and Life,* by Dr. Hugh T. Kerr. Ask them to keep a record of anything they do not understand. Then arrange a conference with each person who reads it, so the meaning can be cleared up.

And emphasize that study of the great beliefs of Christians should continue on and on. One may go on learning in our religion, as he does in science, literature, and so on.

IV
BAPTISM

THE AIM of this lesson is to lead the boys and girls to a better understanding of the meaning of baptism, and of its relation to the Christian life.

In this course, up to the present, we have been working chiefly with material which has a direct and literal meaning—the story of Jesus, faith in him, and the great Christian beliefs. But this lesson and the next deal with a different kind of material. Baptism and the Lord's Supper present some of the deepest meanings of Christ to the Christian heart, through symbolic action.

Suggestions for Lesson Procedure

APPROACH TO THE LESSON. Ask first for the memory work, the Apostles' Creed. And if questions were carried over from last period you may wish to take them up today at the beginning of the period.

As an approach to the lesson itself, you might ask whether the pupils know of any societies or clubs that have an initiation. Ask for description of one or two. But keep this brief, as a point of contact merely, and do not let it monopolize the period.

INITIATION. Have the first two paragraphs read. If possible, use descriptions of initiations, already contributed by the pupils, to furnish further illustration of "acting out a meaning."

Then ask for the third paragraph to be read. Stay on the word "symbol" until the pupils are clear as to its meaning and can use it. If you need further illustrations: a man lifting his hat is a symbol of paying respect; raising a white flag is a symbol to show that armed forces are surrendering; throwing confetti is a symbol of great fun and rejoicing.

Then you are ready to consider some of the meanings which baptism itself symbolizes.

GOD'S SPIRIT. The purpose in this section is to help the boys and girls to know and feel that the Spirit of Christ, God's Holy Spirit, is our Helper. The "Christian quest" is not a lonely one, as if we did all the seeking. Your pupils may still be too young to appreciate the deeper insights into the meaning of the Spirit. But you have the opportunity to make a permanent association in their minds between the visible act of baptism which they will often see, and its symbolic meaning that God's Spirit comes to dwell in the hearts of his children.

Ask that this section as a whole be read before it is discussed. Then you might request that books be closed, and ask such questions as these:

"If you say a person has the spirit of Christ, what does that mean?"

"What are some of the things that that person would be likely to do?"

"What do we mean by the Holy Spirit?" In the discussion here, teach the pupils to say "he" and not "it," referring to the Spirit as a Person.

"When the minister baptizes a person, what does he say?"

"When the minister baptizes a person, of what is that a symbol?"

Then you might ask that Acts 10:44-48; Acts 19:1-7; and I Corinthians 12:13 be read. Point out in each case that baptism and the coming of the Spirit are joined together. You may need to add something of this kind:

When the Holy Spirit came to people's hearts in those days, sometimes the people were so filled with new power that they began to speak in a language they had never used before, and to do other remarkable things. The leaders of the church were thankful for the new power, but they taught the Christians to understand that God sends his Spirit into our hearts to cause us to live a new life, rather than just causing us to speak a new language.

To show the point more clearly, you might use such passages as I Corinthians 12:27—13:1, which shows that love is the best gift of the Spirit; and Galatians 5:22, 23, telling the kind of things that are "the fruit of the Spirit." But whatever the trend in the discussion, before you leave this section, summarize in some such way as this:

God's Spirit is in our hearts, ready to help us live as we should, if we ask him. The water coming upon the person in baptism is a symbol of his Spirit coming into our hearts.

You then are ready to pass to a consideration of four things which the Spirit's coming to the hearts of his children means; that is, to four further meanings of baptism.

OUR CLEANSING. The section may be read, and discussed as seems necessary. The symbolism of cleansing is rather obvious to us, but be sure it is plain to the pupils. You have opportunity to stress the change of spirit, or regeneration, in the Christian when God's Spirit comes to us.

OUR INGRAFTING. The purpose of this section is to carry the thought one step further. Not only does the Spirit come into the hearts of the children of God; but, in the maturer language of the church, one is baptized as a sign and seal of the fact that he becomes a part of the church which is the Body of Christ.

Have the section read. If you should find it is difficult for the pupils to transfer the idea of "grafting in" and connect it with spiritual experience, you can emphasize the fact that baptism is the initiation when the Christian becomes one of a great company who have the same Lord, the same faith, and the same purpose in life. He is not a solitary Christian, but he is one of a great multitude. Thus he has two of the most powerful aids: the Spirit in his heart, and a surrounding, strengthening society who are a fellowship in Christ.

THE COVENANT AND OUR ENGAGEMENT. These sections stress two sides of the idea of the pledge. The covenant lays emphasis on God's pledge to us, while "our engagement" lays emphasis on our pledge to God in the presence of men.

Have the section on "The Covenant" read. See that the discussion brings out the idea that baptism symbolizes God's pledge to us.

Have the section on "Our Engagement" read, and see that the discussion here brings out the contrasted idea of our pledge to God, when we are baptized.

THE BAPTISM OF LITTLE CHILDREN. This section may be read as individual paragraphs. Simple questions will show whether the meaning is clear; such as, "Who are 'children of the covenant'?" "Why do we call them that?" "Who makes the pledge when a baby is baptized?" You will wish the pupils to understand, first, that the four meanings of baptism which have been studied are the same whether a child or an older person is being baptized. And then you will wish them to understand clearly what the two points of difference are.

In closing the lesson, you might like to teach the class the answer to the question, "What is baptism?" in the Shorter Catechism.

V

THE LORD'S SUPPER

THE AIM of this lesson is to help the boys and girls to know how the Lord's Supper came to be, to understand and appreciate certain of its meanings better, to relate the Lord's Supper to their own everyday lives, and to prepare for and partake of the Communion more worthily.

Through the previous lessons of this course we have taught our pupils that upon their profession of faith in Christ, they are to be admitted to the Lord's Supper. Thus, to some extent at least, they should already be prepared to regard this sacrament as occupying a most holy place in Christian experience. Already it should seem to them a high privilege, and not a mere incident in the life of the congregation.

Some of your pupils, no doubt, have looked forward for months, or even years, to the time when they may partake of this sacrament. Many children of the covenant rightly regard this as a supreme privilege of church membership. They eagerly anticipate the day when they may commune with their parents and friends at the Lord's Table. That eagerness, where it exists, constitutes a degree of readiness for today's lesson.

Others, without that background or for some other reason, may regard this sacrament more casually. It is your privilege today to help them to understand and appreciate better, an action which they may have considered commonplace. So far as you can do that, they will have advanced that much in their readiness to use this sacrament as a "means of grace."

Suggestions for Lesson Procedure

APPROACH TO THE LESSON. First take up any topics from previous lessons held over until today. If any of the pupils did not know, at the last period, whether they were baptized in infancy, ask whether they have that information now.

You may wish to say that baptism and the Lord's Supper are called "sacraments." That word first meant a pledge, or an oath of loyalty. Remind them of the last lesson, in which they studied baptism as a symbol. Ask what a "symbol" is. You might then say that the Lord's Supper is a symbol, also, and that we are to think of it today.

YOUR FIRST COMMUNION. You can probably make a point of contact with their own personal experience by the material on their first Communion. Ask for the reading of the section. Encourage discussion of plans for, or memories of, their first Communion. If possible, tell them the date of the Communion service that follows the time when profession of faith is likely to be made by members of this group.

The Last Supper. Ask for the reading of the section. Ask that the New Testament account of the institution of the Lord's Supper be read. These accounts are given in Matthew 26:17-30; Mark 14:12-26; Luke 22:7-20; I Corinthians 11:23-26. Select the one that seems best suited to your group.

Discussion should be restricted as far as possible to clearing up meanings immediately connected with the sacrament itself.

Today. You might begin this section by asking for recall of the things done when we have the Lord's Supper in the church. Have this section read a paragraph at a time, and encourage brief discussion of each paragraph. The purpose in this section is twofold: first, to be sure the pupils know what the outward acts of the Communion service are. If your church has a certain way of celebrating the Communion, you should acquaint your pupils with your own custom, at this point. And second, you have opportunity here, indirectly, to prepare them to participate reverently.

Remembering Jesus. From this point to the end of the lesson, the material is intended to quicken insight into the meaning of the Lord's Supper, and through this insight to suggest ways of worthily preparing for and participating in the Communion.

Have the entire section read. Pupil questions will probably show whether further explanation of details is needed. Then you may wish to go back over the section, and say the same things in your way, more simply still. Observe, for example, that you could bring out the same ideas in a slightly different manner. For instance:

The Lord's Supper helps us to remember Jesus, especially his death. It makes us think of Jesus. But when I meet someone I admire who is fine in spirit, if I have been doing things that are little, sneaky, hateful, suddenly I feel shrivelled up, unclean, in the presence of a noble character. So it is when we remember Jesus. In preparing for the Communion, and at the Communion, look at those sinful things, confess Jesus again. His body was broken for those sins. His blood was shed for them. They *can* be forgiven. They *are* forgiven as soon as we ask God, for Christ's sake, to forgive. That makes the Communion a time of thanksgiving.

COMMUNION WITH CHRIST. Similarly, have this entire section read. Go over the meaning of the word "communion" a second time; the central thought is familiar to boys and girls as "sharing." Then, after any necessary questions, develop in your own words the meaning of communion with Christ.

COMMUNION WITH OTHER CHRISTIANS. The same procedure may be followed in this section. Here you may emphasize in whatever way is most natural to you, that in the Communion we may have a sense of fellowship with all other Christians of every time.

Try to bring your pupils to see, in imagination, the great company of which they become a living part when they become Christians. At the next meeting of the class you are definitely to invite them to enter this fellowship of their own choice. Today, help them to see what a goodly, what a mighty fellowship it is, reaching not only into the past, but on into the future, forever.

Throughout this period you will wish to keep in mind that at the next meeting, the work of the unit is brought to a focus by asking for decision.

In the interval make it a point to talk personally with your pupils, in so far as you have not already done so, inquiring whether they are ready to make the decision next Sunday. Read the next material early in the week, so as to have fresh in mind what the pupils are invited to do in making decision.

VI

DECISION

THE AIM of this lesson is so to lead the boys and girls that they will decide to make profession of faith in Jesus Christ as their Lord and Saviour, to commit all of life to him, and to enter the full privileges and responsibilities of church membership.

In the five preceding lessons we have been leading up to today. It is our hope and prayer that in the period today, each member of the group who has not already done so, will reach his decision to profess faith in Christ and become fully a member of the church. It is well to proceed as if this would be the only opportunity we shall ever have to ask these boys and girls to come to the decision.

To Read Before You Meet the Class

There are deep places of the human soul which no one has the right to try to enter uninvited. And if we are permitted to go in, it becomes us to remember that we are on holy ground.

It is so with the soul of any boy or girl. That person is householder of his own inward domain. We enter, if at all, as guests, and only with his consent. And when are these things ever any more true than when we wish to speak with these, our younger friends, about the disposition and committal of a whole life, with all its hidden bypaths of conflict and temptation, with all its aspirations so delicate as yet that one will scarcely speak of them even to his bosom friend; with its dreams so fragile that he himself is half afraid to voice them even to God, as if in the uttering of them they might fly away to become only a common cloud!

In this hour these boys and girls, "ours" as we call them, will stand at a dividing of the way. Prayer and toil we have spent for many a week, looking forward to this day. With the perspective which a few added years give us we know that the High Road opens before them, in that little bit of time. And we are eager, it may be passionately eager, that the choice may be the choice to commit all to Jesus Christ as Saviour and Lord.

And yet, having done all we could to prepare, and having committed our case to the Father whose will we seek to do, we still must remember that we are seeking to enter those deep places of the self in a boy or girl where no one may go until the door is open from within.

If there should be reticence, reserve, embarrassment, in anyone in the group, we must respect that. There can be no forcing of these doors. It may be that a decision is nearly ripe, but that the time has not yet fully come. We shall hope otherwise, and we shall expect readiness. But if some decision is not ready, we shall beware of pressure for winning that decision, beware of it as we would of a deadly plague.

And we shall guard, as best we know how, against entrapping these boys and girls in any situation where they must choose between hypocritical dishonesty of spirit, and embarrassment. Especially is this to be watched in the use of the suggested prayers. As you read them you will observe that each one is so placed that it can be read aloud for the sake of knowing what it contains; but its *use* as an actual prayer is to be made in silence if at all. Thus the group is not asked to "say" a prayer which, it may be, some members of your class will not be ready to pray genuinely as a prayer.

Assured, then, that we shall respect the rights of privacy in the hearts of our boys and girls, we may go to the church confident that we are on the highest mission a child of God can carry out—that is, to act as an ambassador for Christ, presenting the cause and the call of the Saviour of the world, and asking boys and girls with lives to invest, to choose him as Lord and Master forever. You might well read II Corinthians 5:14-21 as part of your preparation of spirit.

Suggestions for Class Procedure

APPROACH TO THE LESSON. As an aid to starting the period easily and naturally, two illustrations of "making choices" are given in the first section. The first paragraph may be read by one of the pupils. Unless there is evident desire for discussion, ask another pupil to read the second and third paragraphs.

You might ask whether any of the pupils have had to make choices such as Janet and Robert did. In the discussion, quickly bring out the fact that wise choices cause one to grow so that he can be entrusted with still more important decisions. Show that one wise choice helps us to make another choice more wisely, as when we decide to keep up with homework for school, and then it is easier to decide wisely about going places on school nights.

But keep the discussion brief, limiting it, say, to five minutes. Then make the transition, perhaps by some such comment as this: "Today we are to think about the most important choice a person can make."

You might continue with this line of thought, expanding it still further if you think wise: The most important choice we ever make is deciding whether we shall become a follower of Jesus for as long as we live. One reason why that choice is so important is that it helps us to make many other choices wisely. After we have decided to become his follower, we shall still have to keep on making decisions about the things we are to do. But often we will remember our Leader, and think to ourselves, "I should not be loyal to him if I cheated"; or, "I was not loyal to my Leader when I said that mean thing about a certain person, and I am determined to make it right as soon as I can"; or if we are tempted to be untruthful in order to get out of trouble, perhaps we remember, "Jesus told the truth, even though he knew they would kill him for it."

If the length of the class period permits, it would be well to read to the class some *brief* account of the Crucifixion and the Resurrection. But before you plan to use passages for this purpose, calculate carefully the time that will be needed, and see whether enough time will be left in the period for the rest of the lesson. *It will defeat your purpose for the day if you let anything keep you from finishing the lesson.*

But if time allows, you might introduce the first passage by saying, "Before we begin to think about our choice today, I want to read you two stories. The first one is to help us remember, today, that Jesus had to make a choice, and when he had made the choice, he stayed by it to the end, and died for us so he could carry out his choice, for our sake." Then read Mark 15:22-37. You might say, next, "Jesus died for us, but that was not the end of the story. Let me read you a second story, to help us remember that Jesus lived again, and is still living." Read Luke 24:13-35. And you might add, "This is the Jesus whose Spirit is inviting us today to make the most important choice we can ever make."

IN OUR RELIGION. Ask for the reading of the first paragraph. Ask, "What choices were made for us when we were small?" Such things as "Taking us to church," "Taking us to church school," "Helping us to know Jesus," and so on, may be mentioned. But keep this brief.

The central things to be impressed here are, first, that parents and others helped us to know God and Jesus; but, second, no one else can choose whether we shall trust Christ and follow him. Only we ourselves can do that.

Then have the second paragraph of the section read.

THE INVITATION. Have the first paragraph read. This gives a natural opportunity to stress any points in the previous lessons which still need explanation to make them clear to your class.

Then have the next two paragraphs of the section read. If you think it necessary, you might remind the class that such and such persons in the group have already made profession of faith. And if any have told you earlier in the quarter that they desire to make profession, you might remind the group of that fact, and express the hope that still others will do so today.

Read the last paragraph of the section yourself, asking the pupils to follow the reading. If necessary, repeat the matter in your own words.

A FOLLOWER OF JESUS. In this section and the next, it probably is better for you to do the reading, asking each pupil to follow closely in his own book.

Sum up the section, perhaps by saying, "When we decide to make profession of faith, the first thing we are deciding is, 'I mean to be a follower of Jesus.'"

You might continue, "You will remember that in our first lesson of this quarter we studied about followers of

Jesus. A follower of Jesus is one who keeps on learning from Jesus, and from his teaching, how God wishes us to live; and a follower of Jesus is a person who tries, all his life long, to live in that way. We become his followers when we take him as our Lord and as our Saviour. To take him as our Lord means we are deciding that *he* is to be the one whose teaching we try to obey in our living every day. To accept Christ as our Saviour means that we ask God for Christ's sake to forgive all our sins, all the wrongs that we have ever done; and we ask him to keep us more and more from doing wrong, and to help us more and more to live as Christ taught us to live."

Then ask those who are ready to do so, to say in their hearts, not aloud, but as a prayer, "I take Christ as my Lord." And ask those who can, to follow the printed words and pray them silently as you read the prayer in the fourth paragraph beginning "He is my Lord—."

Similarly, ask those who are ready, to say inwardly, not aloud, "I accept Christ as my Saviour," and ask them to pray silently as they follow the words of the prayer which you read from the last paragraph of the section, beginning "I need a Saviour every day—."

A MEMBER OF THE CHURCH. Proceed in the same manner with this section. Read the section, with any comments that seem desirable. Summarize, so that the two decisions stand out: deciding to be a follower of Jesus, and deciding to be a member of the church by one's own choice.

Then ask those who can, to pray inwardly, not aloud, as they follow the words of the prayer which you read, beginning "O God, I see—."

My Decision. Ask one or more pupils, now, to read this section. At the completion of their reading, ask those who can pray the prayer as their own, to do so silently, following the words as you read the prayer.

Then ask those who are ready to make profession of faith in Christ as Saviour and Lord and to ask admission to the Lord's Supper, to give you their names.

If there still remain some members of your group who are not ready to make profession of faith, it is very desirable that you should see them privately as soon after today's lesson as possible. Again let us urge: No pressure! But be sure the invitation itself is understood. Perhaps you will find that some relatively slight obstacle stands in the way, and that it can easily be cleared up. If there is still unreadiness, lead the person to think of each succeeding day as an opportunity to make the decision. But be certain no boy or girl has occasion to feel he is considered "stubborn" or unwanted in the group if he is not yet ready to decide.

Part Four

FOR THE PARENTS

Your son or daughter brings this book home as part of a course he is studying in preparation for church membership. You are invited to read the entire book so that, as far as possible, you may enter fully into his thinking as he prepares for, and consummates, his great decision to profess faith in Jesus Christ and assume the responsibilities of church membership.

The Preface will show you the plan of the book. After the course at the church has been finished, there are seven lessons for home reading and study. The young persons who have been in the class with the minister are asked to carry on this study and reading at home, on their own initiative, but they may need your help with some of the lessons. Perhaps these suggestions will assist you. But in any event you are asked to think with, and talk with, this member of your own home during a time which should mean very much for all his later growth and experience.

This material is divided so as to correspond with the seven brief chapters for home reading.

I

IN TRAINING

To the Parents

THE AIM of this lesson is to lead boys and girls to understand that when we profess faith in Jesus Christ and enlist as members of his church, we become citizens of the Kingdom of God, and as long as we obey the laws of that Kingdom we grow as Christians; to lead them to desire that growth and to determine that they will achieve it.

The Kingdom of God is the rulership of God, his sovereignty over the hearts and lives of men who acknowledge it. Jesus is the Messiah, the Christ, the Anointed of God. One of the basic passages to show the relation of these things to the church, is Peter's confession. "Thou art the Christ," that is, the Messiah, the anointed Deliverer, "the Son of the living God"—that was Peter's confession. "Upon this rock," that is to say, upon this confession of Jesus as the Christ, the Son of the living God, "I will build my church"—that was Jesus' ever-memorable reply. And there, with his acknowledging of Jesus as the Christ of God, the Kingdom of God had come to Peter; Peter had taken upon himself the sovereignty or rulership of God the Father as revealed in his Son. This Messiahship and Sonship, "flesh and blood hath not revealed it unto thee, but my Father which is in heaven." This acknowledgment of Jesus as the Christ, the Son of God, is the foundation rock upon which the church is built; and surely it is one of "the keys of the kingdom of heaven" given in that same breath. (Matthew 16:13-19.)

The Kingdom of God has to have a society within which to find expression. That society is the church. And growth for the Christian comes, not merely by being busy with church activities and "good works," but *by being a member of the church who inwardly and outwardly is obedient to the law of the Kingdom of God.* This is the conception which this course tries to put into terms that boys and girls can manage.

The "means of grace" are means by which the Spirit of God kindles the soul and leads it on with "grace upon grace"—or, as we might put it now, into ever-increasing spiritual growth. These means of grace are especially the Word of God as preached and read, the sacraments, and prayer. The sacraments were considered in the pastor's class. Consideration of the Word of God and of prayer as means of growth is given in a separate lesson on each, as well as frequently elsewhere, in this home study.

Helps for Home Study

The capitalized words at the head of the following paragraphs refer to headings in the home study material where your help is likely to be needed.

THE KINGDOM THAT NO ONE SEES. In reading Matthew 16:13-19, the following questions might be considered. What did Jesus ask his disciples? Why do you suppose he asked such a question? (To find out what people were thinking about him.) Why should he ask, "Whom say *ye* that I am?" (To find out what his disciples thought about him.) What was Peter's answer? When Jesus replied to Peter, he spoke of two things which we also often talk about—the church, and the Kingdom of Heaven. What did he say about the church? (Vs. 18; this means that nothing can destroy the church.) What did he say about the Kingdom of Heaven? (If there is difficulty with the idea of "the Kingdom of Heaven" or "the Kingdom of God," read again what is said in the home study material.)

GOING BACK INTO TRAINING. Perhaps questions of this kind would help to make the meaning clearer. Look at the verses read, Mark 14:26-31 and 65-72, and find what Peter said to show he thought he would never break training. (Vs. 29, 31.) What did "denying Jesus" mean in this story? (Vs. 65-71; Peter's saying he did not know Jesus though he really did; claiming he was not a follower of Jesus though he really was.) What difference would this make to Jesus? (When Jesus' life was in danger, a friend and follower was "going back on him" in order to get out of danger.) How did Peter feel about what he had done, as soon as he had time to think about it? (Vs. 72.)

Questions of this kind may help to bring the meaning home to us today: How could a boy or girl deny Jesus today? (Act like the crowd to keep from being talked about. Use specific examples—such as cruel Hallowe'en jokes, cheating at school, joining the crowd in teasing a cripple, etc.—and ask if these would be denying Jesus.)

Then summarize. Make it clear that if a Christian grows careless and breaks training, Jesus would want to know, "Do you still love me?" If we are ashamed of breaking training (repentant), and keep on loving Jesus our Leader, we can be altogether certain God forgives, and trusts us still. We can begin again, forgiven and trusted. Emphasize the point that whenever one breaks training, it is still his privilege to begin again to keep training, and God our Father longs for this from his children.

II

OUR FATHER'S WORD

To the Parents

THE AIM of this lesson is to help boys and girls to understand that if we are to grow as Christians, we need to grow in our desire and ability to use the Bible and increase our use of it now; to arouse the desire to do so; and to help them actually begin enlarging their use of the Bible.

In today's study we wish to connect the Bible especially with the thought of God our Father, whose Kingdom we have entered, and whose will we seek to obey as growing Christians. We seek to lead boys and girls to see that there is, or may be, a growing use of the Bible. As a child passes into youth it is time to enlarge his conception of the Bible and his actual use of it.

If your children had the Junior work in the Departmental Graded series, it is probable that they can handle the Bible, physically, with fair ease as far as locating references is concerned. Yet you cannot safely take this for granted. They may need further coaching.

Further, the chapter and verse divisions interfere with the use of the Bible seriously enough to create the necessity for counter-measures, fairly early in the life of a growing Christian. One of the best of these measures is learning to read the Bible by "units of thought." Professor Julian Price Love's book *How to Read the Bible* is excellent for its treatment of this method of reading the Bible. Some of the ideas of that book are incorporated in the pupil's lesson for today. But if you can secure a copy of the book itself, it will repay study.

Helps for the Home Study

OUR FATHER'S BOOK. "Revealed" means uncovered, unveiled; God has unveiled his mind to us in the Bible. "Inspire" means to breathe in; God has "breathed in" his truth to the men who wrote the Bible.

As Psalm 119:9-16 is read, ask: What question was the writer of this poem asking himself? (Vs. 9.) What was the place in which he found the answer? (The Bible; point out that in this Psalm, expressions such as "thy word," "thy commandments," "thy statutes," etc., all mean the same thing—the Bible. How many such terms are in this passage?) What attitudes did this man have toward the Bible? (Last three verses.)

A GROWING USE OF THE BIBLE. Stress the point that a growing Christian learns to read the Bible for himself; that we all need teachers if we are to understand the Bible as well as we are capable of doing; but that using the Bible for ourselves is one of the very best ways of growing in our ability to understand it. Here we are trying to get our boys and girls past any notion that they must always have a "teacher" in order to be able to use the Bible themselves.

GETTING BETTER ACQUAINTED. This section and the next are the heart of the matter for today; we are considering a growing use of the Bible, and here ways are suggested for making a growing use of the Word of our Father.

KEEPING A CENTER. When this section has been read, you have opportunity to emphasize the point that Jesus Christ is the "center" of the Bible; that is, the Old Testament looks forward to him, and the Gospels tell the story of his life, death, and resurrection. In that sense the Gospels are at the center of the Bible; and a growing Christian will wish to grow constantly in his understanding of them.

This lesson naturally leads one to undertake to do what he has been discussing, that is, start getting a growing acquaintance with the Bible as a book which one will use for himself in some of the ways already suggested. For example, (1) Read Luke rapidly during one week; (2) the same with Acts. (3) Do exploring reading in Psalms, or Ruth, or Esther, or Jonah, or Genesis. (4) Draw up a plan combining several or all of these, to be talked over each week for a definite time, say three or six months.

III

OUR FATHER'S WILL

To the Parents

THE AIM of this lesson is to help boys and girls to see and understand what the law of the Kingdom of God is; and to arouse their desire to find ways of expressing that law more and more adequately in their own living as growing Christians.

They probably have hazy conceptions of the profound differences between the Old and the New Testaments. And before they can grasp the meaning of "God's will" or "law" for our lives, they need some quite elementary distinctions between the two Testaments. Otherwise, if they seek to grow in their use of the Bible, they may be led either into new perplexity or into an unchristian use of the Bible. For example, they may become perplexed to know how they should regard some of the laws of the Old Testament; or, rather more likely, they may consider all the divine injunctions as being upon exactly the same plane.

So we attempt to study with them "the law of the Kingdom of God" in such a way as to help them grasp some fundamental distinctions between the will of God as expressed in the Old Testament, and his will as expressed in the New.

In the Old Testament we constantly meet the idea that the laws of God are imperative, that all of man's welfare depends upon his keeping of those laws.

In the New Testament we constantly encounter the teaching that law has been done away, and grace has taken its place. We are under grace, not under law; Paul never tires of this great theme. Nor should we ever lose sight of it.

How then can we rightfully speak of any "law" in the Kingdom of God after Christ has come? We may so speak if we remember *what* this "law" is, and *why* it can be called *"law."*

What it is, is plain in Christ's teaching. The "Great Commandments" are a twofold law of love, toward God and toward the neighbor. As Paul puts it, "love is the fulfilling of the law," and any commandment we can think of is summed up in the one which bids us "love thy neighbour as thyself." (Romans 13:8-10.)

But why is love in any sense to be considered law? Essentially for the reason that love, in the fulness of its New Testament sense, is the basic principle upon which human society and the universe are founded. It summarizes the character of God and it constitutes the only basis upon which human personality can thrive. It is "law" because it is written into the nature of things so deeply that no human will can get it out. Keep that law, that is, use it in living, and the best gifts of God to men are released to us. Break it, and life closes in upon us, slowly it may be but very surely, starving us, mangling us, destroying us. "Civilization" today is the only commentary one need cite to show what breaking this law does to men. In the last analysis, though, we cannot "break" this law. We choose whether we shall permit it to make us or break *us*.

We owe it to younger lives to toil at the task of helping them to see this, using every device at our command. For here, in the "law of love," is foundation rock on which to rear a life that cannot be shaken to pieces. Here is "the will of God" for men.

And grace is *God's* love in action, through the Cross redeeming us who are being broken by our sin of not-loving with all its fateful consequences, restoring our souls, taking us back into the society whose one law is this law of the Kingdom of God.

Helps for the Home Study

WHAT IS OUR FATHER'S WILL? Emphasize especially the second and third paragraphs, showing that we cannot dip blindly into the Bible in seeking God's will but must know how to use its different parts. For instance, show that we cannot now go to the book of Leviticus and regard it as God's will for the way we worship in the Christian church.

THE TWO PARTS. Be sure it is seen that the Old Testament gives God's will for his people who were "in training" before Christ came, and that some *but not all* of the Old Testament is "out of date," that is, is not binding upon Christians.

GOD'S OLDER WAY OF TRAINING. In this section try to relate the entire Old Testament to the thought of God's will.

Together you might find the Leviticus references; read a few verses from each chapter cited; stress how important these ceremonial laws were to the Jews, but that they are "out of date" for the Christian. Proceed similarly with the paragraph on the "civil law." Emphasize that the moral law is not out of date. The Ten Commandments are a summary of the moral law.

GOD'S NEWER WAY OF TRAINING. Draw the contrast between giving laws touching everything people did, and giving one law. Emphasize the point that growth comes when we keep this law. Stress also the point that just because the law of love is concerned with loving, the New Testament could not give us detailed "laws" for every kind of situation and problem. For example, it could not tell us how to act in streetcars or buses, or on trains, or while driving an automobile, or when talking over a telephone—for these things did not then exist. But we can find the way to express the spirit of love in all these situations.

IV

OUR FATHER'S WORK

To the Parents

THE AIM of this lesson is to help boys and girls to understand that the church is the Body of Christ, through which the law of the Kingdom of God is to be expressed; to see that each member must do his part if this Body is to function as it should; to see something of what the young Christian's part is; and to advance in growth in some of these ways.

The Christian is like the coupon on a railroad ticket— "not good if detached." Of course he is no Christian at all if detached from his personal relation with God through Christ. But neither can he be much of a Christian if detached from living participation in the church, which is the visible Body of Christ.

The Christian cannot live in isolation either from Christ or from other members of the living society of which he is the Head, the church. And we had best take that saying, "they cannot live," quite literally. Apart from a living relation to Christ *and his church* we shrivel up in spirit until there is little left in us which merits being called life.

The conception of the church as the Body of Christ puts stress upon the necessity that each member be a *functioning* member; he must work at his part in the life of the whole, both for the sake of the whole Body and for his own sake.

This double result of individual faithfulness in participating in the work of the church cannot be emphasized too greatly. A working church is a growing church; in a growing church individual members grow more readily, and as individual members grow the church thrives—so it goes, each kind of growth stimulating the other.

But there are counterfeit forms of participation in the work of the church, spurious forms that wear the appearance but lack the reality. Think how often an individual will receive the benefits and privileges of the church, but will accept none of its responsibilities. See it always in kindness, but nevertheless see it: These are parasites, living on the life stream of the church, contributing nothing in return, draining its strength, often the most critical of critics, static in their own growth, and bringing no greater strength into the parent organism upon which they feed.

No quick and easy measures will heal a disease of this kind. But preventive measures are possible. Working with youth in the church, we can help them to begin taking their part now, as soon as they enter into the complete fellowship of the church.

THE BODY OF CHRIST. You might find I Corinthians 12:12-31 and read it together. Pause only briefly to explain terms that are not familiar, for you wish the line of thought as a whole to stand out.

Next read I Corinthians 13 together. Show that Paul is urging love ("charity") as the controlling spirit in the Body, in contrast with jealousy and lack of teamwork.

Then in your own way sum up the thought, showing that the church is the Body of Christ, with love as its law.

KEEPING OUR PLEDGE. The purpose here is to connect a young person's thinking and his ideas of his responsibility, with the pledge taken when professing faith. There is excellent opportunity now to associate the pledge made on that occasion with a consideration of some of the ways that pledge can be carried out.

V

OUR FATHER'S WORSHIP

To the Parents

THE AIM of this lesson is to lead boys and girls into growth through better understanding of and more worthy participation in worship.

As young Christians they need this experience of worship with the congregation, both for their own growth and for the sake of the church of which they are members. Yet there may be difficulties. In *some* of those who have attended since they were children, there are habits of inattention which may block their growth in the ability to profit by the service.

But this worship by the Christian congregation is central in the life of the Christian church. It is an act of the congregation as a whole, presenting itself before God. And if a child delays too long in coming to the conception that "I belong there because I belong to God," he has to that extent begun to cut himself off from growing into the sense of being part of a greater Christian fellowship of all sorts and conditions of men. If we tacitly assume it is right for him not to do so until he is a little older, we unintentionally nourish the making of another solitary-minded Christian who misses much of the meaning of "The Church."

Helps for the Home Study

THE SERVICE. You might study together the order of worship in your own church. With reference to each step or part in the service, discuss the two questions mentioned in the second paragraph of this section in the home study material. Then show that at least four elements are found in the service: prayers, preaching, giving, singing.

THE PRAYERS. Look up Philippians 1:3-11 in the setting indicated in the home study material. Consider the prayers as offered in your own church's order of service, pointing out values at every possible place. Try to create reverent appreciation of this part of the service in your own church.

THE PREACHING. When the section has been read, discuss such points as need it in your own situation. You might find it possible to sit together in the church service soon, taking "mental notes" on the sermon so as to be able to recall the outline or the train of thought, and later talk it over.

THE GIVING. Point out that giving is sharing both in work and in worship. "How may I give my offering so that I worship through giving?" Would remembering what Jesus said in Matthew 25:34-40 help us to worship? Would remembering sick, lonely, needy people help us to worship? Would prayer to God that he would use what we have given help?

THE SINGING. If possible have at hand a copy of the hymnal used in your congregation. Examine the pages in the hymnal showing how the hymns are classified. Call attention to the fact that the hymns express the great themes of the Christian religion, just as the Confession of Faith or the Shorter Catechism do. And if you know stories about any of the great hymns, these will help to enlist interest.

VI

OUR FATHER'S FRIENDSHIP

To the Parents

THE AIM of this lesson is to help boys and girls to grow in their understanding and experience of prayer.

Prayer is at the heart of the Christian's experience of God. The first of the Great Commandments bids us love the Lord our God with all there is of us—heart, soul, mind, and strength. It is perfectly in place to be reminded often that acts of the Christlike spirit toward our fellows are acts of love toward God. But surely there is a love of God which, however much it acts, is not always in action toward man but "turns again home" to be replenished, and rests quietly in the Presence, expressing love in any language of devotion which the soul can use. It is such acts that comprise the higher reaches of prayer. Prayer is communion with God.

Certainly it includes asking. But if it is all and only asking, the soul is too busy to let God share with us some of the gifts which he waits to impart.

Certainly it includes confession. Without that the soul, sooty with the traces of its dismal choices that day, takes no look at itself in the mirror of God, and goes away uncleansed. Yet if prayer is occupied with our sin and only with our sin, however sinful we be, we have not yet taken the best way to let sin be driven out. For the clear, loving, frequent gaze at the Face of him who loved us and gave himself for us helps to drive out the love of sinning, dispossessing it by a stronger love.

Helps for the Home Study

SHARING OUR THOUGHTS WITH GOD. After this section has been read, you might show that what you have just been doing in thinking out beyond the words of the great prayer, is an example of sharing our thoughts with God.

WHAT THOUGHTS MAY WE SHARE? Let the different "kinds of thinking" in prayer stand out, reading some of the Scripture cited.

At the end of this section, you may find it helpful to use this outline; this is what you have just been considering:

Thinking of God *Thinking About Ourselves*
Thanksgiving *Confession*
Adoration *Petition*

Thinking About Others
Intercession
Action

LISTENING. In this section, guard against two possible abuses of the practice of "listening." The thing we really want to do may come to the surface strongly in these moments, and we may suppose God wishes us to do what we only wished approval for doing. Or quite in opposite fashion, we may suppose that if we really do not want to do something, we can follow God's will only by doing that thing.

A GROWING FRIENDSHIP. Stress the fact that there is no one set pattern for praying. In true prayer, our spirits are free as at no other time in our experience. If we find help from any source in our prayer, that help must not bind us, but rather aid us still more in attaining freedom of soul in our communion with God.

VII

OUR FATHER'S KINGDOM

To the Parents

THE AIM of this lesson is to help boys and girls to see that good and evil are in age-long conflict in our world; to grow in their confidence that the Kingdom of God will be victorious; and as citizens of that Kingdom to take an increasingly worthy part in that struggle.

During times such as these or any other, we owe it to boys and girls to help them form a philosophy of life which enables them to see beyond the present, to catch sight of a longer struggle of which our turmoil is only an episode, and to anchor their hearts in the strong confidence that the Kingdom of God, being stronger than any Kingdom of Evil, will prevail and be triumphant. We want them to root life deeply in the unshakable faith that as Christians, no matter how the game looks at any given moment, they are on the side where victory will finally rest. And we want them to live in such a manner as to bring that victory nearer

The Christian, building his philosophy of history on the Scriptural teachings concerning the Kingdom of God, can be quietly confident of the ultimate outcome of the struggles which fill our world. In that confidence, he can turn to the commonplace task which the next hour holds, shutting his eyes to no hard facts around him, but knowing that if he does his job well he has helped, ever so little though it be, to answer the prayer, "Thy kingdom come."

Helps for the Home Study

THE TWO KINGDOMS. After this section has been read, be sure that two chief ideas stand out: two kingdoms are in conflict throughout the whole world, but the long struggle will go in favor of the Kingdom of God.

A PARTNERSHIP. Bring out the idea of partnership with God, and of God giving the victory which we alone could never win.

WHAT CAN I DO ABOUT IT? Here you come to particulars—helping your own son or daughter to see the "stranger," the "prisoner," the "sick," the "hungry," and so on, within their own surroundings. Together, you and he might find the climax of Christian living by daily seeing and responding to the persons in your own environment who call upon you for Christian living!